PERSUASION

ANTHONY McLEAN

A ... IDE

in 2014 by Icon Books Ltd,
Omnibus Business Centre,
39–41 North Road,
London N7 9DP
email: info@iconbooks.com
www.iconbooks.com

New Zealand
by Allen & Unwin Pty Ltd,
PO Box 8500,
83 Alexander Street,
Crows Nest,
NSW 2065

Sold in the UK, Europe and Asia
by Faber & Faber Ltd,
Bloomsbury House,
74–77 Great Russell Street,
London WC1B 3DA
or their agents

Distributed in Canada
by Penguin Books Canada,
90 Eglinton Avenue East, Suite 700,
Toronto,
Ontario M4P 2Y3

Distributed in South Africa
by Jonathan Ball,
Office B4, The District,
41 Sir Lowry Road,
Woodstock 7925

Distributed to the trade in the USA
by Consortium Book Sales
and Distribution
The Keg House,
34 Thirteenth Avenue NE, Suite 101,
Minneapolis, MN 55413-1007

ISBN: 978-184831-722-2

Text copyright © 2014 Anthony McLean

The author has asserted his moral rights.

Typeset in Avenir by Marie Doherty

Printed and bound in the UK by Clays Ltd, St Ives plc

About the author

Anthony McLean is an Australian persuasion strategist who has worked in the persuasion professions for over two decades. Starting out his career as a police officer, Anthony quickly identified that he had an ability to talk to people. Studying Criminology while working provided a level of practical reality to the theory Anthony was studying that no university degree could ever provide. As a senior intelligence officer, Anthony worked at many high-profile units, including the Homicide Investigation Group and the Special Emergency Response Team – the Queensland Police Tactical Group and Counter Terrorist unit charged with dealing with high-risk incidents requiring tactical and negotiated resolutions. It was in these theatres that Anthony first delved deeply into the science of persuasion.

Leaving the police to pursue opportunities in the private sector, Anthony travelled to the United States and trained with the most cited social scientist in the world in the field of Social Influence, Compliance and Influence: Dr Robert B. Cialdini. As one of only seventeen Cialdini Method Certified Trainers (CMCT) in the world, Anthony has provided real-world persuasion training and strategies to thousands of participants from more than 40 countries. He provides businesses and governments with the tools and strategies to ethically persuade others on a daily basis and breathes practical application into the science of persuasion.

Anthony resides with his wife Robecca and their three loving children Samara, Nea and Ryan on the Sunshine Coast in Queensland, Australia.

To my family. Without you this would never have been possible. To Samara, Nea and Ryan: remember you can do anything and be anyone and I will always love you. To Robecca: thank you for your ongoing support, love and guidance and for teaching me to be grateful.

Contents

Preface

If you have picked up this book, you are looking for one thing: you want others to say 'Yes'! Yes to your requests. Yes to your ideas. Yes to your products. Yes to your proposals. You want people to buy what you are selling or buy into your ideas.

As a persuasion strategist, I see many claims by people suggesting you can learn the power of instant influence. You can take people's words and actions and, as an influence ninja, have your way with them. The one thing they all tend to leave in the fine print or just omit altogether is that much of what they are teaching is their opinion or anecdotal observations. While they claim to have discovered the path that all others can only hope to follow, it's more spin and hype than usable tools and strategies.

The reason I say that is because if it were true I would not be writing this book – because we would already know how to get want we want. Conflict would not be occurring around the world and negotiation would be a redundant skillset. Well, my friend, turn on the news. Businesses close down every day because of a lack of sales or an inability to resolve executive level disputes. Governments battle to engage people to look after their health and drive safely. Parents struggle to get their children to clean up their rooms, turn off the screen and come to the table for dinner.

There is no magic bullet or secret sauce in this book. Instead, this is a practical introduction to the content, strategies, frameworks and tools of persuasion. I thought long and hard about how best to present what we know about the science of persuasion and decided that, rather than provide long, verbose chapters, I would break it down into four sections, each complete with short, sharp and relevant explanations of what you need to know to become an effective persuader.

If you are an 'intuitive', a person who can just change the behaviour of others, this book will provide you with the language and labels to understand what you are able to do. It will provide you with the knowledge to be able to modify your approach when what you have always done no longer works. Most importantly, it will allow you to explain to others and teach them what you are able do naturally.

If you are new to the field of persuasion and are looking for a place to start, this book will provide you with the knowledge, skills and operational language to commence your persuasion journey. The work in this book is rooted in science, not opinion; therefore there are structure, research and case studies beneath each point, some brought to the surface and others simply referenced for your ongoing development.

If you need to sell something, lead people, drive change, problem solve, negotiate, provide advice, work with others, resolve conflict or pretty much do anything else with people, this book will be an invaluable introduction to the field.

The purpose of this book is not to provide you with every framework, strategy and tool available. As a practitioner I know overloading you with information is as counterproductive as not knowing the tool exists in the first place. Instead, I will provide you with practical, useable tools and techniques that will enable you to start your persuasion journey.

In my opinion, the reason why this book is so important is because persuasion is one of those words that is frequently used in business, yet many people do not truly understand its meaning and, therefore, the distinction between persuasion, influence and manipulation is all too often blurred. A simple premise of this book is to explain it for you so you can do it.

SECTION 1:
Understanding

Section 1 is dedicated to providing you with the underpinning knowledge and understanding of what persuasion is and, probably more importantly, what it is not. In this short section we will develop your factual knowledge of persuasion. To do this, we will provide you with knowledge of terminology, language and specific details relating to the history and development of persuasion as a discipline.

The purpose of this first section is to ensure you grasp the meaning, nature and importance of persuasion. This level of comprehension alone will start to differentiate you from your colleagues, competitors and leaders.

The reason this is important is because in recent times, and certainly with the growth and pervasiveness of the internet, we as a society have started use the word 'persuasion' in many instances without any clear idea of what it means to persuade someone.

1. Yes

It is an attitude, not just an answer!
Changing the minds and behaviours of others is an achievable goal. You need to believe this first before you read any further. If you need to take a second, do so and re-read it.

 If you feel you cannot change someone's behaviour, then you probably will not be able to. However, if you believe it is achievable, you will at least give it a go.

Persuasion is as much about possessing a persuasion attitude as it is about the preparation, planning and tools used.

A skill you need
In a world where our daily challenges are more complex, resources remain scarce and resistance to change is high, persuasion is a skill everybody in business needs to understand. This is because rarely does behavioural change just happen. In each situation there is a trigger which results in a series of messages and exchanges between the parties involved: each designed to persuade the other to change their behaviour or beliefs about a person, activity or thing.

Albert Einstein suggested that problems cannot be solved by the level of thinking that created them. New ideas and actions are required to solve problems: the big and the small. The problem with new ideas is they often require people to do things differently, to change not only their mind but also their behaviour.

While it is consistently said that people resist change, it is probably more accurate to say that much of what people do is driven by habit. Habits that have been learned over a period of years live deep within our brain and they tend to resist change.[1] This is because the brain likes to conserve energy, and the easiest way to do this is to undertake repetitive and comfortable tasks and turn them into habits, thereby reducing the brain power required to process new tasks. At any point where we ask people to deviate from these ingrained habits, we are asking them to expend energy to make a decision, something the brain prefers to resist in exchange for the way it has always done things, relying on habit and preserving, not expending energy. John Maynard Keynes hit the nail on the head when he said: 'The difficulty lies not in the new ideas, but in escaping from the old ones.'[2]

Therefore, as we embark on this journey, realize that some people will not like your ideas: some out of a resistance to change and change alone; others because they don't like you or your idea. To succeed you have to convince them to say 'yes' or to at least consider what you are proposing.

Implications for you

- People may resist your persuasive approaches but a willingness to change their mind and behaviour is a large part of the skill of persuasion.

2. Mystery

Why do we do what we do?

Let's start with a mystery. Why would normal people electrocute someone they have never met?

Some of you may be familiar with the Milgram obedience studies conducted in the 1960s; Yale University psychologist Stanley Milgram tested the obedience of participants by asking them to deliver electric shocks to someone they had never met in order to help them learn. In the experiment, participants delivered what they perceived to be the equivalent of lethal levels of electric shocks because they were instructed to do so. Why?

Here's another one. Why would masses of people drink from a vat of poison and lay down to die?

That's exactly what 918 members of the Peoples Temple, a religious group under the direction of Reverend Jim Jones, did in 1978 in Guyana. Believing their compound was about to be set upon by authorities, members lined up to drink from a vat of poison at the request of Jones. Why?

Finally, why would a person give away their life savings to someone they had never met?

Victims of the Nigerian 419 scams (419 being the section of the Nigerian Criminal Code dealing with fraud) have done exactly that. In the scam, victims are enticed to provide a small amount of money in the promise of greater returns later on. Delays are always encountered, more money is required to release the funds and the unsuspecting victim is persuaded to send more until eventually they run out and all communication ceases. Why?

The answer in part to each of these mysteries is persuasion, and we will unpack each one in the book.

The question of why we do the things we do has puzzled mankind as long as we have bartered, traded and interacted with each other. Think about questions such as:

- Why did your boss say 'yes' to employing a person who is clearly not the best candidate for the job?

- Why did you buy that new pair of jeans when you already have five just like them at home?

- Why did you agree to volunteer for something you never really cared about?

- Why do we buy, sell, give away, agree to or concede to anything?

The answer is persuasion!

Some of these, especially the 419 scams and Jonestown Massacre, are examples of harm being done to others. Positive examples are equally available, such as reforms to energy use in the home, safer driving practices, better health-related decisions, more volunteers, increased voter numbers, successful negotiations, more sales and so on.

IF YOU REMEMBER ONE THING

There are positives to be gained in understanding persuasion, and one of them is a greater ability to protect yourself from people using some of the tactics on you.

Implications for you

- People do things that from an outsider's perspective would be considered irrational. Throughout this book, understand that we are dealing with conscious and subconscious processes.

- Understanding the cues that trigger these behaviours will allow you to persuade others and protect yourself from unwanted persuasive requests.

3. History

Persuasion: where does it come from?

Just as you are pondering the question today of how to nudge your boss to accept your new proposal, how to sway your colleague to change tack on a particular activity or perhaps even how to convince your kids to eat their vegetables, these fundamental questions of human behaviour have been asked since the time of ancient Greece, 2,500 years ago. But the reason the 5th century BC is so important to the field of persuasion is because it represents the first acknowledged period where this curiosity moved from passing individual thought to sustained attention by scholars focusing on rhetorical communication.

Therefore, as you read this book, take comfort in the fact that you are not alone. As humans we have long been fascinated and perhaps frustrated in our ability to get others to do what we want. This fascination has been driven as much out of our ability to gain compliance as it has been out of our inability to have others assent to our requests.

It has, however, been long understood that if you want to change someone's beliefs, you need to communicate with them, not *at* them, and invite them to make a decision of some sort.

To persuade people, you need to communicate with them and invite them to make a choice or decision. It is at the point of the decision that the communication ramifies into behaviour.

A move from art to science

In every society we have marvelled at those who can effortlessly persuade. Equally, we are somewhat bewildered by those who cannot. At work you may look in wonderment at a colleague's seamless approach to having others consider, adopt and execute their ideas. Yet when you try to replicate their actions, it quite possibly ends in tears, perhaps those of someone else but, as is more often the case, probably your own.

Therefore, it is not surprising that people on both sides of the ethical fence have searched long and hard for the secret to changing the behaviour of others.

By way of example let's consider Dale Carnegie. Here was a man who was able to learn from his surroundings and observe the attributes and actions that made people more influential. In his 1936 award-winning book *How to Win Friends and Influence People*,[3] arguably for the first time, Carnegie was able to take his experience and aptitude and hone his tradecraft into a carefully constructed manuscript for others to follow. An artisan, Carnegie took real-world observations and used what he learned to impact on the behaviour of others.

But persuasion is not just the purview of philosophers and artisans. Around the same time as Carnegie, scientists were also becoming increasingly interested in how people behaved socially: how they made decisions and how they influenced each other.

Although texts focusing on social psychology first emerged at the start of the 20th century with William McDougall's 1908 text *An Introduction to Social Psychology*,[4] the field really started to expand around the time Kurt Lewin immigrated to the United States from Germany in 1933. Through his research, Lewin became universally recognized as the founder of modern social psychology, pioneering the use of theory, experiments and hypothesis testing to place a discipline around the influences that impact our beliefs and behaviours.

A groundswell of research soon followed and there was a concerted drive to understand the nature and causes of individual behaviour in social situations through science.

This led to Milgram's obedience studies and the surprise findings that all participants were willing to deliver a 300 volt shock to the 'learner' in response to getting a maths problem wrong and, even more surprisingly, that 65 per cent of 'teachers' continued all the way to administering the highest level of 450 volts.[5] Dr Philip G. Zimbardo's 'Stanford Prison Experiment'[6] highlighted the impact of conformity and roles within the social world with implications being drawn as far as Abu Ghraib prison. Dr Robert B. Cialdini conducted his systematic investigation into the six

Principles of Persuasion,[7] providing a roadmap for modern, lasting and ethical change, which saw him become the most cited social scientist in the field.

These early pioneers inspired the throngs of researchers who today explore every nook and behavioural cranny to gain a better understanding of why we do what we do and how best to influence it.

In completing this journey from wonder, artistic interpretation and now science, today more is known about how we function as people than at any other time in our past. Research is continually driving our understanding forward, but there is a need to put this research into practice. Therefore, the focus should be on taking this science and making it immediately useable in the challenging interpersonal, time deprived, digital world we find ourselves in today.

However, regardless of how hard we try, not everyone will apply what we know in exactly the same way. This is where art yet again meets science. Science can tell us what we know about people and decision-making processes, but it is your flair, innovation and ability to present the options, ideas and proposals that will add to your success. Hence, there is plenty of science available to you; however, you need to bring the art to the execution phase.

Implications for you

- Because persuasion is rooted in science, we are able to learn it, explain it and teach it.

4. Sector

Public or private sector? Is a different approach needed?

For centuries public officials have struggled with the concept of moving people and effecting change through public policy. Their solution historically was one of legislation, regulation, sanction and penalty. Why? Perhaps it is because laws are easily defined. While not always popular, laws are able to be debated, refined and written into legislation. This means they are able to be understood and therefore adhered to by the people they seek to govern. Perhaps it is because governments traditionally try to move the masses rather than focus on a person-to-person method of communication and behaviour change.

The mistake businesses made early on was to follow governments' command-and-control structures and seek to gain compliance from staff by clearly defining roles, functions, activities and performance measures, penalizing those who deviated from the accepted norm. Driven by the bottom line, however, businesses quickly realized they were able to use 'carrots' to incentivize their staff: using rewards and bonuses to motivate them, rather than always having to swing the stick. Unfortunately, this approach led to a 'get ahead at all costs' type of attitude that promoted a 'greed is good' mentality, which, of course, gave rise to questionable behaviour and equally questionable ethics.

But ever-evolving with cross-functional teams, joint ventures and intercompany partnerships, businesses realized there was a better way still. Managers realized that if they could persuade people to change their approach or attitude without force or incentives, it would reduce conflict, increase adherence and reduce costs, which would subsequently increase profitability. This gave rise to the new pioneers of business, the behaviourists.

These visionaries communicated with people. They attempted to change their behaviour by having them make informed judgements. They created situations that made their audience more receptive rather than imposing their will upon them.

In turn, governments are now also slowly realizing that changing behaviour through science – e.g. getting people to pay their taxes on time because of the way they are notified in a letter[8] or to use less energy because of the way the billing information is presented[9] – is a much longer-lasting and therefore sustainable approach.[10]

Therefore, regardless of position or sector, the practicalities of how to persuade others without having to rely on hierarchical power, compliance rooted in regulation or sanction or any type of unethical or underhanded approach is critical for longer-term success and getting people to do more with less.

CASE STUDY

In February 2011, HM Revenue and Customs (HMRC) in the United Kingdom, supported by the Behavioural Insights Team, conducted a trial to ascertain the impact of sending letters to tax debtors to encourage them to pay their taxes.

The traditional approach had been to remind the debtor of the debt, demand payment and ultimately fine them if they did not comply.

The new approach targeted 140,000 debts worth £290 million. The letter told the debtor that the majority of people in their area had already paid their taxes and reminded them of the importance of doing so to ensure local services were able to be maintained.

This approach achieved a 15 per cent increase in repayments over the standard formal letter approach, demonstrating the value of using behavioural research in the public sector.[11]

Implications for you

- Regardless of sector, behavioural research can be applied to change people's behaviour.

5. Universality

Professionally, personally or socially?

The concept of universality dictates that the applications for persuasion are virtually limitless. Regardless of the environment in which you need to move others – such as professional settings, within groups, bodies you volunteer with, social groups you participate in and even at home – persuasion is always available to you.

 While it is important to be aware of cultural implications and variances, in the main everything we explore here is universal, i.e. it applies across cultures.

It all comes down to communication

Persuasion is all about human-to-human (H2H) contact and all the variables and challenges that brings with it. Clear, concise and purposeful persuasion will allow you to:

- Change attitudes and beliefs toward you or your proposal

- Present a speech to gather support, votes or donations

- Deliver a marketing campaign or advertisement

- Lobby support for a change in policy

- Convey a message to a resistant audience

- Encourage visitors to take action while on a website

- Modify workplace behaviour

- Hear 'yes' more often!

Modalities

The universality of persuasion is not just limited to the groups or locations you are delivering your message within. It is also important to realize that universality also applies to the scale of your messaging, including delivery:

- One to one
- One to a few
- One to many
- One to the masses.

It always starts with one because persuasion is a human endeavour. It is about people. Therefore, even when a brand, business or government engages its community, it is done at the hands of people.

Similarly everything we discuss in this book can be used when persuading:

- In writing
- Orally
- Using a blended approach.

Implications for you

- Persuasion occurs in all facets of business and at home.

- Persuasive messages can be delivered across many modalities (written, oral, digital).

- The universality of the tools allows for both intra- and intercultural application.

6. Operational language

A need for a common language

Already in the preceding chapters we have touched on some critical words and phrases that you must understand. In many books on persuasion it is assumed that you understand what these words mean. Mainly because in your daily life you use words like *persuasion*, *influence*, *manipulation*, *compliance*, *negotiation*, *coercion* and *inducements* very frequently. It is assumed that you have a level of knowledge and possess your own working definition for each of the words, which indeed you do. In creating your own understanding, however, you have also established your own perceptual filters and lenses through which you consider and use each of them, rightly or wrongly.

Here is the question: is your definition of the word *persuasion* the same as your colleagues', your boss's or even your partner's?

History tells me no. Not by a long shot.

Let me explain why. I have been involved in the persuasion profession for over two decades, and the one thing that I can always rely upon is that if I ask a room full of people to turn to the person next to them and come to agreement on the difference between the terms *needs* and *wants*, they have no problems quickly doing so. This agreement is not only achieved within their pair but also more broadly across the entire group.

Collectively they have a shared concept or operational definition of the meaning of the words and how they apply in their context.

However, if I ask the same group to come to an agreement on the difference between *influence* and *persuasion*, the task becomes much harder. Even if a pair discusses, compromises and agrees, I guarantee that they will not have the same answer as the pair next to them. In over six years of delivering Dr Cialdini's 'Principles of Persuasion Workshop' and delivering keynote speeches on the topic, I have never had a group unanimously agree on the difference between *persuasion* and *influence*.

 The words *needs* and *wants* are used daily, just as the words *influence* and *persuasion* are. Why then can we come to agreement on one but not the other?

Everyone has a shared understanding of what *needs* and *wants* mean. They are fundamental to social functioning. However, even though the terms *persuasion* and *influence* are equally used on a daily basis, we do not have a shared or common understanding of their meaning.

In my opinion, the confusion occurs mainly because the word *influence* has been diluted through a gross overuse. In general the word has been extended to mean so many things. A quick online search reveals 128,000,000 hits for it, ranging from definitions, Cialdini's book, professional development courses, social campaigns, marketing companies, strategy consultants, political donations, hypnosis and many other things.

Therefore, with the expansion of the term to cover all aspects in the interpersonal, digital and marketing worlds, the lines have become blurred as to its meaning and application.

From the top down

To reach a definition of persuasion, we must start with the broader concepts and move down to the more specific.

Social influence

Elliot Aronson stated in *The Social Animal* that social influence at its broadest definition is the influence people have on the beliefs and/or behaviour of others,[12] and this in effect becomes the working definition for the field of social psychology.

Therefore, it may serve to think of social influence like an umbrella. Within the Social Influence Umbrella there are many tools, strategies and methodologies for changing an individual's thoughts, feelings, attitudes and behaviours. Each of these tools, strategies and methodologies are like ribs of the umbrella allowing it to open and to achieve the goal of influencing beliefs or behaviours.

Influence

More commonly used than the broad term of *social influence* is the word *influence*. In modern business 'influence' is commonly taken to mean the capacity to have an effect on someone or something. It is both a product and a process. As a product, influence is tangible: something that can be measured. As a process, influence is something that is able to be used to create that outcome.

Under this very broad definition many methods, tools and strategies can be used to have an effect on behaviour; hence why the word influence is so commonly associated with anything relating to behavioural change, perceived or real.

Achieving influence

In looking at how influence occurs, we most commonly hear about major behavioural change that is achieved through the use of the 'carrot' or the 'stick'. The carrot is where someone is incentivized or induced to change their own behaviour, whereas the stick is where coercion is used to enforce the desired behavioural change.

Rewards, bribes, threats, coercion, obligation, promises, inducements, rapport building, active listening, role modelling, mentoring, etc. can all have an effect on someone's behaviour; therefore, we recognize them as tools of influence and each makes up a spoke of the Social Influence Umbrella.

However, there are some problems with this very broad definition, namely:

- It is inclusive of both ethical and unethical practices.

- The tools able to effect behaviour change are numerous; therefore, anything that effects change can conceivably be called a tool of influence.

- Many tools can demonstrate change, but they lack empirical evidence as to their effectiveness and ability to be replicated in a standardized manner across varying cultures and contexts.

- Some tools and their associated effects are not long-lasting.

 In 2009, Volkswagen Sweden initiated the Fun Theory Award, where it looked at whether fun could change behaviour for the better. Entries included Piano Stairs, in which a set of subway stairs located next to an escalator were converted into piano keys. The point of the exercise was to see if people would take the stairs if they were seen to be more fun rather than the less healthy option of the escalator. During the period of review, 66 per cent more people chose the stairs over the escalator, demonstrating that fun can change behaviour.

The winner of the competition was surprisingly a speed camera entered by Kevin Richardson from the United States. Richardson's entry converted a speed camera not only to record and penalize those who were speeding but also to photograph those abiding by the speed limit. In recognition for their law-abiding behaviour, these drivers were entered into a lottery to win cash prizes taken from the fines of the speeders. Ingenious, right?

According to data provided by Volkswagen, speeding dropped by 22 per cent during the time the camera lottery was in place.

For more information see: www.thefuntheory.com.

But did the change last?
On the face of it, it seems fun can change behaviour. But the real question is: what happens when the lottery speed camera or the piano keys are removed? Will behaviour return to normal?

Longevity of change
If behaviour returns to normal, e.g. people take the escalator and not the stairs, or they resume speeding, we can see that behaviour was affected in the short term. Therefore, by definition, they did influence the behaviour of others.

But what are the broader implications of change that is not long-lasting?

If the behaviour change does not last, then we can say that the influence tool did have an impact on behaviour, but it did not change the underlying belief system of the person. For example, if people took the piano stairs because it was fun, but they didn't take stairs elsewhere when walking to their destination, the concept of piano stairs hasn't changed their attitude toward healthy choices in general; it has not changed their beliefs. Similarly, if people slowed down when the lottery speed camera was in place but sped up again when it was gone or continued to speed elsewhere, then it can be said the camera did not change their attitude toward speeding in general.

If the change achieved is only behavioural and not belief-based, influencers will need to constantly come up with new and novel ways to get people to do things, and this will become expensive and perhaps a little hit-and-miss with some tools working and others not.

Perhaps this is why governments have historically relied on sanctions and penalties as their preferred method of behaviour change. Due to their defined nature and lack of necessity for continual change, updating, innovation and ultimately expenditure, a government can rely on this approach with some degree of certainty as to their cost and effectiveness.

Conversely, what would be the impact on the advertising industry if it were able to effect belief-based change through its campaigns? Would this reduce the need for advertisers' services? Therefore, do advertisers encourage short-term behaviour change through gimmicks, inducements and fun, rather than deep-seated attitudinal change, to keep themselves in a job?

Longer-term sustainable change

Leaders from all sectors know that the challenge is not only behavioural change but long-term sustainable change. The goal, therefore, is to achieve change in the short term but also change that lasts in the longer term because of attitudinal change in the mind of the recipient.

US President Dwight D. Eisenhower said: 'I would rather try to persuade a man to go along, because once I have persuaded him, he will stick. If I scare him, he will stay just as long as he is scared, and then he is gone.'

Leaders need to look at sustainable and ethical ways to engage and motivate people to change.

Persuasion

Persuasion, therefore, is the process whereby one person communicates a message to another in an attempt to change the way that person feels, thinks or acts in relation to something or someone.

Returning to our umbrella analogy, persuasion is another spoke of the Social Influence Umbrella, one that is based on over 70 years of research and business application.

 Ishmael is a productive and innovative member of your team who has stated openly that he is interested in challenging himself and developing his skills. An opportunity has arisen for someone to move into a new position under a different project leader to help deliver a complex yet important project for the company.

You approach Ishmael with this opportunity, and he

flatly refuses to consider it because of the project leader he will have to work for.

In a conversation with Ishmael you confirm his development goals and aspirations. You confirm the type of position he believes will afford him these opportunities. You advise Ishmael that you have come to him first because you knew of his desire for extension and that your next step will be to provide the opportunity to all staff. You tell him that this is the only development opportunity you know of for the remainder of this year and that, with someone having to leave the team to fill it, opportunities for the remaining staff will be restricted as the position will not be backfilled.

You then review the role and function of the new position, having Ishmael confirm that it meets all of his criteria and that professional development is still important to him.

Finally, you state that while the reporting lines may not be ideal, this could be a career-defining opportunity and your door will always be open if he has any problems with the new leader.

By undertaking this process you identify, confirm and use Ishmael's intrinsic motivators to overcome his singular negative focus on the leader. You change the way he thinks about the new role by drawing his attention to the opportunity, the meeting of his goals and criteria, the professional development involved and the scarcity of it coming up again.

You then ask Ishmael a second time if he would like to take the role and he says 'yes'.

The above approach did not involve begging, coaxing or coercion. It did involve a careful process of preparation, proper framing of the various points and effective presentation of the message to Ishmael so he could consider it differently.

Firstly, it should be noted that persuasion is not always seeking to achieve wholesale attitude change. At times it may only seek to modify a single belief or value. Secondly, persuasion is not necessarily a one-off communication, although in some instances it may be. More likely, change will occur over an extended period of time with numerous interactions in order to achieve the desired outcome.

Ultimately, remember that the goal in making any persuasive request or structuring a persuasive appeal is to have the receiver of the message, i.e. the persuadee, move in your direction.

THINK ABOUT IT

Think back to our example of the piano stairs and speed camera lottery: persuasion has occurred if commuters continue to use the normal stairs over the escalator when the piano stairs are removed. This is because their attitude toward healthy choices has been modified.

Similarly, persuasion has occurred when the lottery speed camera is removed and vehicle speeds remain at the reduced level. In this instance, the attitude of the drivers toward speeding has been modified.

Therefore, in seeking to achieve behavioural change, ask yourself: are you looking to change a particular behaviour? Or are you seeking to change the way the persuadee sees, thinks or feels about something or someone – i.e. to change their attitudes and beliefs about the topic or person – and, as a result, achieve long-term behavioural change?

For some people, it is enough just to change a behaviour right here, right now. That is influence. For others though, you want to change the behaviour by changing the attitude of the persuadee; *that* is persuasion and that will make sure it sticks.

Persuasion is more than just sales

Persuasion is widely and incorrectly perceived as just a sales or marketing tool. While very effective in these fields, it is also used every day by leaders in business, law, medicine, human resources, social work, workplace rehabilitation and so on.

Think of any role that requires the change agent to ethically alter the attitudes and behaviours of others for their own or social good, and we could just as easily call these 'the persuasion professions'.[13]

In fact, a study in the United States identified that those designated as 'wise managers' stated they spent 80 per cent of their time 'persuading others'.[14] This is not a surprise because if the manager is able to engage with their staff and persuade them, they no longer need to push because the staff have altered their attitude toward the person, activity or thing and their behaviour becomes self-driven.

THINK ABOUT IT What was your first impression of buying items over the internet? Depending on your age, this may have been a major change or just something everybody does. If buying online was a major change for you, it is likely it took you a while to warm to the idea, maybe even buying pizza online long before you paid your utility bills over the internet.

How do you feel about not having cash money at all and simply using an app on your smartphone for all transactions?

These are examples of movements in attitude change from resistance to acceptance. As a whole, society has been persuaded to move to online banking technologies and away from labour-intensive processes.

7. Ethics

Manipulation is a type of social influence that aims to change the perception or behaviour of others through underhanded, deceptive or even abusive tactics. You only have to ask people if they have ever been or felt manipulated and they usually have a strong emotional reaction to the question if they have. This is often because they felt they were moved to do something that was against their own self-interest and that they lost something as a result: money, status, self-esteem or perhaps all three.

How does manipulation differ from persuasion? Manipulation is doing something *to* someone: by virtue of your ability to influence someone else's behaviour, you have them do something against their own self-interest. They lose, you win.

Persuasion is doing something *for* someone: by virtue of your ability to change their behaviour, you have the persuadee do something that benefits themself and probably you as well. Often the change would not occur without you presenting your message in a particular way.

 Manipulation is doing something *to* someone; persuasion is doing something *for* someone.

Bernard 'Bernie' Madoff pleaded guilty in March 2009 to running a Ponzi scheme that cheated investors out of billions of dollars. Madoff was subsequently convicted and sentenced to serve a 150-year prison sentence. At the time, the scheme was considered to be the biggest financial fraud in US history, with thousands of victims.

Madoff was a highly respected, well-established financial expert. He helped to found the NASDAQ stock exchange and served as its chair for a term.

Unlike many Ponzi schemes, Madoff did not offer exorbitant returns, instead promising moderate and consistent earnings.

Like all Ponzi schemes, Madoff needed initial investors that would be quickly followed by the next rung of investors. The second rung paid the first rung, and Madoff would take his percentage. As the scheme continued, new investors needed to be continuously added to pay the previous rungs.

Like all Ponzi schemes it eventually became unsustainable and failed.

The ethical point here is that Madoff knew his investments were a scam. He knew it was unsustainable and that people would lose their money, in this case totalling $65 billion.

Not only was he manipulative and secretive, he lied and fabricated all sorts of documentation to his clients and the US Securities and Exchange Commission (SEC).

In this circumstance, Madoff was doing something *to* people not doing something *for* them!

In exploring the issue of persuasion, we must pay some attention to the ethics involved in such activities.

Your Personal Ethics Statement

Ethics is a critical component to any Persuasion Strategy. While many organizations have ethics statements, you as an individual must have an ethical approach to your persuasive activities.

Your Personal Ethics Statement is a critical tool in how you will go about changing the behaviour of others. In a few short steps you should be able to define your Personal Ethics Statement, but remember that this is your personal view. It is based on your ethics, morals and context.

Ask yourself the following questions:

Why is it important for me to be ethical?

This is the core question that will determine the way you go about executing your persuasive strategies.

What do I consider to be unethical behaviour that I therefore would never exhibit?

This question establishes the baseline of behaviour you will not cross. It defines the backstop against which all other behaviour can be measured.

What situations might I encounter that will challenge the above?

This highlights any situations where you may be in a place of perceived ethical risk and allows you to become vigilant to them to minimize exposure.

Collate your responses into a sentence and place this on your résumé or website for all to see. At a minimum have it ready at your next job interview should you be asked a question about ethics or honesty.

The Reasonable Person Test

As an ethical guide, simply ask yourself the following question to see what an average, reasonable person would think:

If I walked up to a random person on the street and told them what I have done or was planning to do, what would they say?

If you are not comfortable with the answer, then this is probably your ethical guide in undertaking that activity.

THINK ABOUT IT

What do you think a reasonable person would have said to Bernie Madoff had he explained the intricacies of his Ponzi scheme?

The world sat up and took notice when the story broke that Madoff's sons Mark and Andrew turned their father in to the authorities, knowing he would spend the rest of his life in jail.[15]

There will, of course, always be exceptions. However, as a general rule, we are looking at whether you are able to explain your actions to such an extent that a reasonable person would understand why you did something. Remember, they don't have to like what you have done, as is the case when you make difficult or unpopular decisions, but they must be able to understand why you did what you did and be okay with your decision-making process.

It's all about choice

A key aspect of persuasion is the requirement for the persuadee to make a decision. It is all well and good to present the information in a manner that engages the persuadee; however, if they are not called upon to make a judgement or decision then nothing will occur.

This decision must be made in light of the facts and free from bias, manipulation and lies. The reason being, if someone is forced into doing something, this is what we call *coercion*. While their behaviour may be impacted and they may do something they otherwise would not have done, their attitudes and beliefs will remain unchanged. Similarly, if someone goes along with the group, when they sit in a meeting and say 'Sure, I will do that', just to fit in, this is called *conformity*. Again, they may appear to be modifying their behaviour in the meeting, but as soon as they leave the room they revert to their previous state because they only ever said 'yes' to fit in with the social norm.

Therefore, when we persuade, nudge, sway or change

someone's behaviour, we are looking deeper than just the behaviour itself. To impact on the behaviour and not change the way the recipient sees or thinks about something is *influence*.

To change the way they receive a message, think about a person, an issue or a thing: this is persuasion. Yes, their behaviour is modified, but it has occurred at an attitudinal level, therefore creating a longer-lasting change. The linchpin then is the making of an informed and active choice to do or not do something that is consistent with and locks in this new way of thinking and acting.

Take five minutes to formulate a Personal Ethics Statement that you can refer to in job interviews, place on résumés or simply live as part of your personal brand.

Answer the following:

- What things will I do to get my proposal, offer or service accepted?

- What won't I do to get my proposal, offer or service accepted?

- Am I confident my actions can withstand the Reasonable Person Test?

- What exceptions, if any, exist to me telling the truth?

- If there are exceptions, am I comfortable with not telling the truth?

- If the persuadee were Grandma, would this change my approach?

Implications for you

- The use of persuasion is a personal commitment based on ethics, morals and context.

- Manipulation is doing something *to* someone; persuasion is doing something *for* someone.

- If you are unsure, apply the Reasonable Person Test to assess your situation.

- Persuasion is all about the decision and allowing it to be made free from biases or inappropriate factors.

8. Your operational dictionary

In this section we have started to build your operational dictionary and to clarify the difference between the words we use. Here is a recap of what we've covered so far.

- **Bribery** is the giving of a bribe (such as money or a favour) to a person to influence their views or conduct.

- **Coercion** is where someone is forced to do something they don't necessarily want to do.

- **Conformity** is where someone says or does something to fit in, but they do not really hold the attitude or belief they have stated.

- **Inducement** is where an incentive is given to help bring about an action or desired result.

- **Influence** is about having an effect on someone's behaviour.

- **Manipulation** is having an effect on behaviour through deceptive or abusive means.

- **Obligation** is where someone does something because they think they should, again, modifying behaviour but not changing the way they think about a person, issue or thing.

- **Persuasion** is where someone's thoughts, feelings,

attitudes and beliefs are modified, using intrinsic and/ or extrinsic drivers to modify behaviour.

- **Promise** is where an assurance is given that you will or will not do something, often in return for a desirable view or conduct.

- **Threats** are an expression of an intention to inflict plain, injury or punishment.

SECTION 2:
Preparation and planning

Knowing the tools or how to persuade someone is only half of the battle. To explain, let me use an analogy. A builder has many tools available to them to construct a house. They do their apprenticeship and learn how to use each tool to a high level of proficiency. But just because they know how to use the tools does not mean they will be able to build the house. Usually, they need the architect or the homeowner to give them the plans of what to build where.

Persuasion is the same. Knowing how to persuade is important, but before you start you need to know what it is you are trying to achieve. As we mentioned in the previous section, sometimes it is overall attitudinal change that is required and in other cases it is a single attitude or belief that is to be changed.

We will come to the tools of persuasion shortly, but there are a few things we must do first.

Contrary to popular belief, preparation and planning are not the same thing. Preparation is doing your research. It is about understanding the persuasion environment and those within it. You must understand the paths to persuasion and the hubs and ripples that will be created by any persuasive activity.

Planning is taking your research and coming up with a strategy of how you will achieve your goal or goals.

 Preparation is doing your research. Planning is how you intend to use it.

---

9. Prepare

While it may not seem like it, unspectacular preparation is the key to success in persuasion. You must know who is involved, how they are connected to others, what they think, and understand the environment in which they are required to operate.

To come back to our construction analogy, top quality painters will spend time preparing their site by protecting, sanding, cleaning and taping rather than just opening a tin of paint and throwing it around. They need the right paint, the right colours and the right brushes and rollers for the task at hand if they are to be truly successful. So do we. Let's spend some time *preparing to persuade*.

It starts with research

Research and understanding is the key to success. Digging into and gaining an understanding of the context in which your request will be made and received is critical. You must know what factors and limitations will impact on your request and the possible consequences of them.

In any persuasion activity, if you know more about the persuadee than they know about you, you are at an advantage. This knowledge enables you to know the things you have in common, the people you both know and, importantly, the issues to avoid.

Review your persuadee's Linked In profile, their Twitter

feed, their blog and anywhere else they may have made comments which can give an insight into them as a person.

 Always remember the 'Google Rule'. Before you meet with anyone or any company, Google them to get to know a bit about them. Nothing is as persuasive as showing you have done your homework and made an effort to understand your persuadee.

Here are some other simple research ideas to help gain an understanding of the persuadee and their context:

1. Speak to others: Get a clear picture of the stressors and pressures that are present.

2. Ask questions: Ensure you attend briefings, arrange meetings and, when given the opportunity, ask relevant and insightful questions. Always have two questions at the ready. The reason you should have two questions is that the first question will give you an overview and the second question will allow you to dig deeper. For example:

Question 1: *Can you tell us about any financial limitations that will impact on the project?*

Question 2: *What will be the direct impact on your team?*

Question 1 will give you the financial overview, whereas Question 2 will give you a deeper insight into the impact of these limitations on and the priorities and/or concerns of the persuadee. Here we get an insight into their attitude, motivation and level of interest in the issue at hand.

3. Listen: Listening is different to hearing. Hearing means you have the ability to hear something. Listening is hearing plus understanding what is being said within context. Listening allows you to ask better follow-up questions, and you will learn as much from what is being said as you will from how it is said and, most importantly, what is not said.

When asking questions, it is important that you listen to the answer to the question you have just asked and not be tempted to jump ahead thinking about the next question you will ask.

IF YOU REMEMBER ONE THING A sage piece of advice I was given early in my career was: if you are talking you cannot be listening. Therefore, effective persuaders know when to talk and when to be quiet. As my father used to say: 'You have two ears and one mouth. Use them accordingly.'

---

4. Get social: Review your persuadee's social footprint. Look at their online profiles, associations, memberships and the informal groups they belong to. Look at the comments they make online and get an understanding of their likes and dislikes. Take note of who influences them and the issues that are pushing their buttons.

See who they communicate with. Take note of the issues they are facing or commenting on.

Also note the most common times of day they are online, as this may provide an insight into the times of the day or night you might be able to access them later in your Persuasion Strategy.

5. Look up public statements: Review press releases and comments they have made on behalf of their company. Look at any presentations they have made to conferences, special interest groups, etc. and the currency of these presentations.

6. Understand finance: Get an understanding of the financial pressures on the persuadee and their business.

7. Keep up with current events: Review current events, political, financial and social issues that will impact on the persuadee and/or their organization.

Above all, take what you have learned and use it.

Implications for you

- There is no substitute for research.

- Before you meet with anyone, allow yourself time in advance to find out whatever you can about them and the issues they are facing.

10. What

The 'what' comes before the 'how'. At the outset of any persuasion activity you must clearly identify what it is you want to achieve. By failing to define your outcome it is easy to become side-tracked and lose focus.

To assist you in developing a plan, let's consider a number of simple steps.

Step one: establish an Aim for your Persuasion Strategy

Your Aim is what you want to achieve. Establishing an Aim at the outset of your strategy is critical as it:

- Provides structure

- Dictates what is to be done

- Allows for priorities to be developed

- Most importantly, identifies that once the Aim has been achieved the task is complete.

 In articulating your Aim you are defining what you want to achieve.

There are many ways to develop an Aim; one common way

is George Doran's SMART mnemonic, first addressed in the November 1981 issue of *Management Review.*[16] For our purposes, we are going to modify the original mnemonic slightly to read:

- **Specific:** target a specific outcome.

- **Measurable:** quantify how the outcome will be measured in both behaviour and beliefs.

- **Active:** do something.

- **Realistic:** state what results can realistically be achieved, given available resources.

- **Timely:** specify a deadline.

For example, in the case of an internal change management programme, your Aim might be:

To gain the Organizational Development Leader's support for the delivery of a new change management programme by October, allowing it to commence in the next calendar year.

Using the SMART approach, this example breaks down as shown in the table opposite.

Setting a specific and measurable Aim will let you know whether you have achieved it or not. All too often persuaders overpersuade. They over talk. They miss the signals that indicate they have achieved their goal and continue to talk without really listening, thereby damaging or undermining the good work they have previously done.

Specific	Support for the delivery of a new change management programme from the Organizational Development Leader
Measurable (Behaviour)	Delivery of the change management programme in the next calendar year
Measurable (Beliefs)	The OD Leader takes interest and advocates the programme, lobbying executive support
Active	Gain support
Realistic	This Aim is within the OD Leader's scope and area of interest
Timely	Support achieved by October for commencement in January

 Setting a SMART Aim will keep you on track and tell you when you are done.

Implications for you

- Identify what it is you want to achieve.

- Make it specific, measurable, active, realistic and timely.

11. Who

You can't persuade someone if you don't know who they are. By using the PEAK mnemonic you will gain a better understanding of who you really need to persuade and what they stand for.

PEAK = Persuadee + Essentials + Attitude + Knowledge

P = Persuadee

While conducting your research, you must identify the relevant stakeholders that need to be persuaded, those who need to be kept informed and those who are not relevant. Even when seeking to change the behaviour of a group or organization, it always comes down to the key people involved. Two of the key aspects you are looking to uncover are: who is able to make or influence the decision and who is interested in what you have to say.

 To be persuaded, your persuadee must be interested! Interested in you, the topic, the potential or the idea. Think about it: every time you have started to think about something differently you will have been interested in the person, thing or idea. Your attention will have been heightened until the point when you made a decision to act or not.

Disinterested persuadees are fatal to the persuasion process.

When researching the situation, create a Stakeholder Table and each time you encounter a person of interest add them to the table. The categorization is very simple and looks at the interest and decision-making capability of the person (see overleaf).

Identifying persuadees at ABC Corporation

ABC Corporation has a number of sites spread across the globe providing a 24-hour working capacity and diversified operations. Over the past five years all sites have implemented their own autonomous safety systems, which have been contextualized to their physical, legislative and cultural environment. Analysis of the systems has identified considerable duplication of effort and wasted expenditure. The board has decided that a uniform safety system will be implemented across all sites with administration and support to be housed in head office.

The CEO and CFO were key decision makers in the initial scoping phases; however, the execution has now been delegated to the general manager of Site 1, Adrian Li, who was on the Executive Working Group. Due to the linchpin status of Site 1, it has been identified as the initial implementation site.

The processes used and adopted at Site 1 will become

STAKEHOLDER	DESCRIPTION	ACTION
Decision Makers	Decision Makers are those you need to support your request. Some Decision Makers may need only to have their support confirmed; others may need to be actively persuaded. *This is the key column of your table, as Decision Makers are the people with the power to ultimately say 'yes' to your request, proposal or idea.*	Need to be fully engaged in the process and have their needs met.
Indirect Leaders	Indirect Leaders are those individuals with high levels of power who are not necessarily involved or interested in your request. If they are not supportive of your request, some effort may be expended in neutralizing their disagreement to ensure friction is reduced for your Decision Makers. However, if time is short and/or resources are scarce, Indirect Leaders need only be monitored and considered as secondary or tertiary persuadees to be catered for in the execution of the Persuasion Strategy. Be careful not to alienate these stakeholders by unnecessary communication or requests for involvement. *Any leader who is directly involved (they have a high level of interest and a high level of power) will almost always be in the Decision Maker category.*	Need to be monitored and kept informed.

STAKEHOLDER	DESCRIPTION	ACTION
Influencers	Influencers are those individuals who have no real decision-making power but do have some level of influence over the Decision Makers and therefore may have some level of interest. Influencers can be current or former colleagues, friends, siblings and even partners or children. Influencers can become great advocates and vehicles for change while having little or no formal decision-making capability.	Need to be kept engaged and appropriately informed.
Others	Any other stakeholder that has some association to the request. They traditionally have low interest and low decision-making ability. They require minimal effort apart from periodic review to check they have not migrated to another status. Be careful not to disengage these people through excessive or unnecessary communication.	Require minimal effort apart from the occasional status review.

the template for rollout across the other sites starting with Sites 2 and 3. Due to the required change programme, the global human resources leader has been speaking to Adrian Li and guiding his thinking regarding the implementation process.

The other key decision makers in this programme are the global safety leader and the global IT leader.

Here is an example of how the Stakeholder Table would be completed for this scenario:

	Decision Maker	Indirect Leader	Influencer	Other
Bill Smith (CEO)		X		
Jane Gower (CFO)		X		
Adrian Li (GM Site 1)	X			
Farhid Ali (GM Site 2)			X	
Cassandra Ng (GM Site 3)			X	
Jenny Schmidt (Global HR Leader)			X	
Wong Lee (Global Safety Leader)	X			
Ravit Dayan (Global IT Leader)	X			

From this Stakeholder Table we can see that Adrian Li, Wong Lee and Ravit Dayan are the targets of our persuasive activities. There are also a number of influencers who can directly impact on their decision making and some indirect leaders that must be monitored and kept informed.

 If you are struggling to identify the relevant stakeholders, hold a brainstorming session with your colleagues to see how many relevant persuadees you can come up with.

Once you have identified the list of persuadees, then categorize them.

Do not try to categorize the list as you discover each individual, as this will impede the brainstorming process and side-track stakeholder identification with labelling. Come back to categorizing the stakeholders once they have all been identified.

It is also worth noting that a stakeholder's category could change at any time depending on contextual and/or environmental change.

Once you have categorized the list you will then be able to focus on those who need attention (Decision Makers), those who need be informed (Indirect Leaders), those who need to be engaged (Influencers) and those who need to be loosely monitored (Others).

IF YOU REMEMBER ONE THING

An all too common mistake is spending too much time attempting to persuade the wrong person.

It is tempting to spend equal amounts of energy on all stakeholders, but some people deserve and need your attention, and others do not.

The initial task of the persuader is to ascertain which is which.

Beware the time-sapping, energy-sucking bystanders who have no real impact on the decision or person you are seeking to persuade. These are people who do not make it onto your Stakeholder Table yet seek to command your attention.

Charting

There are many ways to monitor the stakeholders you have identified along with their associations with each other. One helpful process is to create an association chart or Persuasion Map. This is a simple process of writing each of the stakeholder's names in a circle and connecting them to others by lines with appropriate labels. This can help to identify connectors or Persuasion Hubs where one person is able to persuade many others. Similarly, it will also help to identify non-essential stakeholders, i.e. those who can take up your time and resources but not contribute to the overall outcome.

There are software tools available to assist with this

type of chart, but it can easily be achieved through the use of some very simple conventions, plus a pen and a piece of paper. The charting conventions for creating your Persuasion Map or Hub are to:

- Colour code the circles to match the categorization (Decision Maker, Indirect Leader, Influencer, Other).

- Draw your circle sizes based on importance: the more important the stakeholder, the larger the circle.

- Label the links between stakeholders by writing on the line.

- Place an arrowhead at the end of the line, indicating the direction of the persuasion (noting that it can be bidirectional).

- Vary your line thickness based on persuasiveness: the stronger the persuasive ability, the heavier the line.

 Take a piece of paper and draw a Persuasion Map listing the stakeholders from ABC Corporation (see p. 56).

Analysis

Now that you have identified the relevant stakeholders and their place in the persuasion landscape, you are able to analyse your Persuasion Map to identify:

- Key persuadees by category (e.g. Decision Maker, Influencer, Leader, Other)

- Barriers and/or obstacles that exist in getting access to the Decision Makers

- Groups (formal/informal) that the Decision Makers are part of

- Persuasion clusters (e.g. groups of Decision Makers or Influencers)

- Where you sit in relation to the Persuasion Map and key persuadees

- Potential paths to reach your persuadee.

From this process you should now be able to clearly identify your key persuadee or persuadees. The Persuasion Map also allows you to identify not only the strongest path to your persuadee but also the many indirect paths that exist to access them.

 A company in the United States has taken association research to a new level by creating a relationship database that lets you use the people you know to connect with the rich and powerful people you do not.

Relationship Science, or RelSci, is the brain child of Neal Goldman and has attracted millions of dollars in investment since its inception in 2010. The RelSci system does not house contact information, instead it highlights the path to your intended persuadee with clean data, making the approach all the more meaningful.

Goldman and his team of hundreds of engineers, editors and data scientists have spent years constructing their network of 3 million profiles using only publicly verifiable information. This requires constantly scraping the web for updates and building rich profiles from thousands of databases. This data has, in turn, been joined to link everyone through past and present employers, board memberships, investments, donations, political involvement, and even siblings, children and spouses.[17]

See: www.relsci.com.

E = Essentials

Having identified your persuadees, you can now set about tailoring your research and undertaking a meaningful and targeted process of discovery, focusing on each of them and their individual circumstances.

This should allow you to identify the essential needs of the persuadee and recognize what is important to them. While there are many ways to ascertain the essentials for each person, here are some simple questions you can ask to identify the key motivational drivers and identify any conflict that may arise:

- Is **meaning** important for them? (Do they need to derive a sense of understanding and significance from things they do?)

- Do they need to feel **secure**? (Are they risk-avoiding or risk-seeking?)

- What **connection** do they need to the project, people or issue? (Are they someone who needs intimate involvement, control and ownership?)

- What **recognition** do they need? (Are they driven by status or are they in a position where recognition is critical to them or their business area for ongoing survival or success?)

- What **action** do they need to take? (Do they have specific things they need to be done?)

- What **motivator** is driving these needs? (Is this an intrinsic motivation or are they being driven by extrinsic factors?)

THINK ABOUT IT You may have the best idea, product or service, but if the persuadee has no need or sees no need for it they are likely to say 'no'. Therefore, overcoming this will become a core element to your Persuasion Strategy.

Of course, if they have a clear need as a Decision Maker or Influencer and what you are proposing is essential to them and their ongoing success, this is a much easier path for you to follow.

Motivation

Motivation is a reason or reasons for acting or behaving in a particular way. It is why someone does something.

It is worth noting that people will do what you ask, and feel good about it, as long as they believe they are acting in their own best interests. Therefore, uncovering their essential needs, wants and desires and understanding what is driving them allows you to present an option that satisfies these essentials. By doing so, the persuadee will more than likely move in your direction because they see they are acting in their own best interests and not yours.[18]

Therefore, think of motivation as a cycle. Any behaviour that achieves a persuadee's goals and satisfies their essential needs will, in turn, create more and similar behaviour because they want more.[19]

The research into motivation is aimed at answering the question of why people do things or, perhaps, why they do not. Numerous models and theories to help explain why we do things have been developed, such as:[20]

- **Instinct** Theory of Motivation: people are motivated to behave in certain ways because they are evolutionary programmed to do so.

- **Incentive** Theory of Motivation: people are motivated to do things because of external rewards.

- **Drive** Theory of Motivation: people are motivated to take certain actions in order to reduce the internal tension that is caused by unmet needs.

- **Arousal** Theory of Motivation: people take certain actions to either decrease or increase levels of arousal.

- **Humanistic** Theory of Motivation: people have strong cognitive reasons to perform various actions.

What drives you?

In breaking motivation down into its simplest form, let's look at two sources:

- Intrinsic
- Extrinsic.

Intrinsic motivation is when we undertake a behaviour because it is internally rewarding. We undertake the task or behaviour because of who we are and what we think of ourselves. It makes us feel good and we do things because we want to. Behaviour is not undertaken for attainment of any specific external reward.

Extrinsic motivation is when we undertake a behaviour because it is externally rewarding. We undertake the task or behaviour because doing so will earn us a reward or allow us to avoid punishment or loss.

Advertisers and marketers use Scarcity (see chapter 21), the psychological principle that says we are motivated by things we stand to lose or want because they are rare or dwindling in availability, as a means of triggering the extrinsic motivation for you to take action. They highlight how much time you have left, that a product is running out or that you are in competition with others to motivate you to take action so you don't miss out.

Yes, it is a motivator, but is it more powerful than an intrinsic motivator?

Research suggests not. Intrinsic motivation is known to last longer than an extrinsic motivator. People have more initiative when driven to achieve, they are more satisfied and are, well, more motivated to see the task or action through to completion.

Extrinsic motivators are often people- or issue-centric. For example, I want to lose weight for my wedding (issue-motivated). Once the issue is achieved or resolved (e.g. I get married), then usually the desired behaviour also passes, unless it has become habit (I no longer watch my weight, I just eat healthily because that is what I do). Therefore, extrinsic motivators can be temporal.

Intrinsic motivation, however, it is usually not person- or issue-centric. For example, if people volunteer their time to help animals or people less fortunate than themselves, the sense of purpose or satisfaction does not diminish after saving one dog or working in one soup kitchen.

Why then do marketing and advertising campaigns use the extrinsic motivators so much more than intrinsic?

In my opinion, people who continue just to focus on

extrinsic motivators do so because they are lazy. Extrinsic motivators are easier.

You can easily show people what they stand to lose or use market forces to genuinely create Scarcity or the perception of it. The reason it works is because every organism on earth is bound by Scarcity – if we don't have enough to live we die – so it is an easy card to play to get people to take action.

But it is overdone. Yelling, screaming rug salesmen on television do not motivate me to go buy a rug. All they do is lower the price point of rugs because they obviously have 50, 60, 70 or even 80 per cent mark-up because they are discounting the price by that amount every other week. The frequency and overuse of extrinsic motivators such as Scarcity can and does work against companies, not for them.

Triggering intrinsic motivation is harder though. It takes genuine interaction. It requires the asking of well-constructed questions and the willingness to listen.

The persuader needs to elicit a commitment from the person in order to trigger the motivation, and then this becomes the driver to stay on track.

So the choice is yours: rely on overused extrinsic tools like Scarcity or – if you want to truly master the art of persuasion – learn to ask great questions and elicit commitments to trigger the unending power source within, the intrinsic motivator.

A = Attitude

In the preparation phase it is important to gain a clear understanding of the beliefs, values and attitudes of the persuadee toward the object, thing or person you are attempting to persuade them toward.

To further expand our operational language:

- **Beliefs** are what we consider to be true or probable.
  For example, I believe that some chemicals are entering the food chain through current farming practices.

- **Values** are what we consider to be right or wrong.
  For example, I value sustainable organic farming practices and the effort that is made in following this approach. I do not accept that the blanket use of chemicals is necessary to produce high-yield crops. Therefore, I will seek out and buy organic produce where possible.

- **Attitudes** are a combination of our beliefs about a thing and the value judgements we associate with it.
  For example, my attitude toward organic farming practices is that the effort to source and support organic produce is entirely worthwhile in order to limit the chemicals that enter our diet through the food chain. While I am supportive I am not fanatical, and while my primary choice is organic produce I will buy non-organic products where organic products are not available.

From the above breakdown, you now have an insight into my attitude toward organic farming. If you were attempting to persuade me to assist a chemical company to increase the uptake of a new spraying technique, my attitude is not only relevant but also very important.

If you are attempting to persuade me to buy into a policy change at the office to use less paper, my environmental beliefs may also be worth knowing.

If the policy change you are attempting to persuade me toward is about the allocation of parking spaces to employees, my attitude toward organic farming is not relevant in the slightest.

 Understanding someone's beliefs, values and attitudes on general issues may be relevant to the specific issues you are dealing with. Preparation will guide how deep you need to dig.

Knowing someone's beliefs, values and attitudes on the specific issues you are dealing with is critical for success, as you will see below.

The following are key points in understanding attitudes. Attitudes:

- Are formed by the building blocks of beliefs and values.

- Are more than just our momentary emotional states or moods.

- Are general evaluations, whether favourable or unfavourable.

- Are learned, not innate.

- Precede and consequently influence our behaviour.

- Are the link between what we think and what we do.

- Involve intensity of feeling: they are strong, weak or neutral. They are directed toward a specific thing, person, event, idea, proposal for action or the action itself.[21]

 The stronger our beliefs about positively valued attributes, the more favourable our attitude toward that object should be.

The stronger our beliefs about negatively valued attributes, the less favourable our attitudes should be.[22]

Receptivity

When considering a persuadee's attitude, you need to gain an appreciation of their receptivity and the intensity of their emotions relating to you or your request. If we work on a simple seven point scale this will help to ascertain the level of support or resistance you can expect from your persuadee and allow you to react accordingly.

The seven point scale is broken down as follows:[23]

	Label	Meaning
-3	Hostile	Actively working against you
-2	Strong Disagreement	Strongly disagrees with you
-1	Disagreement	Disagrees with you
0	Indifferent/Apathetic	Is neutral toward your position and needs convincing, either: Informed but does not care Uninformed and needs information
1	Sympathetic	Understands and is interested in your position but needs to be activated
2	Strong Agreement	Already agrees with you
3	Ready for Action	Already showing initiative and working with you

The above ratings are easily translated to this continuum:

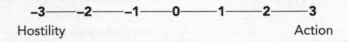

The degree of agreement/disagreement will dictate the response required. In the table opposite, the goal is to move the persuadee from the previous, less supportive state to the one below it, thereby moving them away from disagreement toward agreement.[24]

Therefore, when determining a persuadee's receptivity, understand what they believe to be true or not, how much they value right or wrong, and how strongly they feel about the person, thing or activity being proposed.

	Intensity of Attitude	Action	Persuasion Goal
–3	Working Actively Against you	–	–
–2	Strong Disagreement	Defuse	Defuse the anger or suspicion and commence to build the relationship and trust.
–1	Disagreement	Neutralize	Take someone from disagreement and move them toward apathy or indifference.
0	Indifferent/Apathetic	Crystallize	Get people who are uncommitted to move toward agreement and to see the persuader's point of view.
1	Sympathetic	Intensify	Intensify the weak agreement to strong agreement and subsequently toward action.
2	Strong Agreement	Activate	Look to move them from a supportive attitude to ready for taking action.
3	Ready for Action	Reinforce	Allow them to take action by providing the tools and support to enable action to occur and prevent them from being discouraged through inaction.

Then ask yourself whether you need to:

- Persuade them to acquire a new belief or attitude on a single issue.

- Defuse disagreement.

- Engage them and move them forward.

- Strengthen current convictions.

- Make them resistant to change.

- Discourage backsliding.

- Engage in wholesale change.

 For higher level application, you can add Attitude Intensity to your Persuasion Map using symbols such as these indicating (– – –) working against you, (– –) strong disagreement, (–) weak disagreement, (0) indifferent/apathetic, (+) sympathetic, (++) strong agreement, (+++) ready for action.

By copying the original Persuasion Map, you can then contextualize it and chart different issues or proposals according to receptivity and attitude intensity.

K = Knowledge

The final step in understanding your persuadee is to make sure you are not over- or underselling your request.

Therefore, it is critical to understand just how much your persuadee knows about the issue you are communicating and to tailor your presentation accordingly.

A simple guide is to ask yourself these questions:
1. What do they already know?
2. What don't they know?
3. What do they need to know?
4. What don't they need to know?

 By not understanding what someone already knows or does not know, you can over-persuade – i.e. talk too much when they already understand what you are proposing – or under-persuade – i.e. do not provide enough information for them to make a decision because you thought they already had an understanding of the issues at hand.

While it is a small point, it is crucial to your success.

Reaching the PEAK

By following the PEAK process and answering the questions associated with each section, you will be armed with the criteria to include or exclude information based on who the persuadee is, what is important to them, how they think or feel about your presentation and what they do or do not know.

For any questions that you are unable to answer, this

is obviously where further research is required or at least where caution should be exercised when dealing with the persuadee based on your lack of knowledge around a particular point or issue.

 In conducting your research, it is okay to say you do not know something. But you must find out the answer.

You also need to spend time understanding why the persuadee has previously said or is likely to say 'no' to your request.

Implications for you
Consider the use of PEAK by focusing on the following:

Persuadees
- Categorize key persuadees (e.g. Decision Maker, Influencer, Leader, Other).

- Ascertain the barriers and/or obstacles that exist in getting access to the Decision Makers.

- Determine the groups (formal/informal) of which the Decision Makers are part.

- Establish any persuasion clusters (e.g. groups of Decision Makers or Influencers).

- Understand where you sit in relation to the Persuasion Map and key persuadees.

- Explore a number of potential paths to reach your persuadee.

Essentials
- What are the persuadee's priorities?

- What meaning do they need to derive from the situation?

- What do they need to feel secure?

- What connection do they need to the project, people or issue?

- What recognition do they need?

- What action do they need to be taken?

- What motivator is driving these needs?

- What will their reaction be?

- What will their objections be?

Attitude
- Understand what the persuadee believes to be true or not.

- Find out how much they value right or wrong.

- Discover how strongly they feel (intensity) toward a specific thing, person, event, idea, proposal for action or the action itself.

Knowledge
- What does the persuadee already know?

- What don't they know?

- What do they need to know?

- What don't they need to know?

12. Why

Step two: understand your Reasons for your Persuasion Strategy

Your Reason is why you want to achieve your Aim. All too often people embark on a behavioural change programme or activity without clearly understanding why they are doing it. It is easy to establish the goal posts of what we are looking to achieve, as we have done in step one. But many do not stop to consider why they are doing it in the first place.

This situation can be seen in workplaces all around the world every day, where a big-thinking leader walks in each morning with a new idea or direction for the business. Often they know what they want to do but do not know why it is important for the business or its people. In this situation many ideas are confused, misaligned, cause distress and often run out of steam because they lack clarity and support for the idea.

As a persuader, if you clearly understand your Reason for undertaking the activity, it will be communicated in not only what you say and do, but also in how you say and do it. The other benefits of clarifying your Reasons early are that you can:

- Check alignment with your personal and company ethics.

- Identify if your motivation is driven from emotion or reason.

- Quickly identify with the stakeholders you uncovered in your preparation.

Let's consider the Reasons behind our Organizational Development example:

My Aim	To gain the Organizational Development Leader's support for the delivery of a new change management programme by October, allowing it to commence in the next calendar year
My Reason	To effectively engage staff in the company and increase the overall sense of connectedness as a business

Five Whys

If you are struggling to articulate your Reasons for undertaking this activity, you can utilize the 'Five Whys' technique as a simple tool to determine the root cause for your motivation. The 'Five Whys' is a method of discovery attributed to Sakichi Toyoda, an industrialist, inventor and founder of Toyota Industries. The method became popular in the 1970s and, due to its remarkably simple execution, it is still used today by Toyota and businesses of all sizes to understand and solve problems.

The 'Five Whys' was originally designed to identify root causes of problems or track cause and effect. We are going to modify the standard approach slightly while still maintaining the essence of the tool by asking the question 'why' no fewer than five times. In our circumstances, rather than having a problem and working back to identify its root cause, we are going to look at the persuasive issue and uncover the root motivation for making the request.

Firstly, identify the issue and uncover its nature and source by asking 'why' a minimum of five times.

For example, what is the root motivation for me presenting the following to the OD Leader?

	Persuader
Problem	The change management process needs Executive Support.
Why?	Without it, the programme will struggle and probably fail.
Why?	It will be seen as just another project we force upon staff that was driven from the top down.
Why?	We have a history of piecemeal, reactive programmes and telling staff they must do things.
Why?	We are not strategic enough in our programme planning and delivery.
Why are you doing this?	We are too insular and do not engage broadly enough across the business; hence our programmes are not as successful as they could be.
Resulting Action	I need to engage the OD Leader to ensure we have a whole-of-business approach and do not repeat the mistakes of the past.

THINK ABOUT IT

If you do not know why you are doing something, it is very difficult to inspire others to follow you.

By tapping into your passion and drive for an idea, proposal or service, persuadees are able to see your reasoning and more easily identify with you and your message and are better able to support you.

Simon Sinek addresses the premise of 'people don't buy what you do, they buy why you do it' in his 2009 bestseller *Start With Why*.[25] His associated TED talk went viral because in it Sinek explained that great leaders not only understood why they did something but they were also able to communicate this to others, thereby inspiring them in the process.

I would strongly encourage anyone seeking to persuade others to invest the eighteen minutes and watch Sinek's video: http://www.ted.com/talks/simon_sinek_how_great_leaders_inspire_action.

Step three: Understand your persuadee's Reasons

As we mentioned earlier, people will do what you ask, and feel good about it, as long as they believe they are acting in their own best interests. Therefore, you need to understand why they should care about your request and be able to answer 'what's in it for me?' (WIIFM).

Features, Benefits, Implications (FBI)[26]

Most people in sales have been taught over the years not to focus as much on the features of the product they are selling as on the benefits it provides. In relating this to Sinek's model (discussed in his TED video), it is not so much about what it is, than it is about how it will benefit them.

Most people are happy to talk about what they are proposing or what they will do. These are effectively the features of the product, service or offering. In looking at the features of a proposal or service, there are usually many that can be listed. For example, in implementing our change management process, we can list a number of Features.

Features in and of themselves are required, but, because there are so many of them, they will send the persuadee to sleep if you speak about them indefinitely.

As we mentioned above, most sales people (who are always in the business of persuasion) seek to draw the Benefit out of each Feature for the persuadee. We can do this simply by asking 'so what?' for every Feature.

While persuasive, Benefits are not as good as it gets. As you can see from the table that follows, we are going to repeat the process, asking ourselves 'so what?' to get to the higher order Benefit – or the Implication – you are trying to draw.

FBI = Failure

Here is the critical takeaway for this tool and the thing that will set you apart from many others in the presentation

Proposal	Features (Numerous)	Benefits (Some)	Implications (Limited)
Implement a new change management process across the business	1. Takes a systematic approach to human activities	*So what?* Removes the human related issues from the requirements phase	*So what?* Reduces errors
	2. Provides leadership involvement at every level	*So what?* Better-informed and engaged decision makers are able to make faster decisions	*So what?* Takes less time to make key decisions
	3. Requires ownership by stakeholders	*So what?* Provides scope for autonomy and leadership	*So what?* Provides an opportunity to stand out
	4. Defines communication channels and methods	*So what?* Communication is clearer and more productive	*So what?* Less misunderstanding
	5. Benchmarks across business areas	*So what?* Allows for measurement across business areas	*So what?* Success is obvious

of persuasive requests. If you start talking about the many Features a product, person or process has and then move onto the Benefits, by the time you have drawn the Implications for the persuadee, they have stopped listening or you have run out of time.

IBF = Success

Start with the Implications. Tell the leader that: 'You will stand out from others because your success in reducing mistakes, driving productivity and having everyone on the same page will be visible.'

If we start at the Implications, the persuadee is immediately paying attention. They see why they should be involved because you have drawn the Implications for them. You have reached into the situation and pulled their best interests to the surface.

If they ask, 'How will we do that?' you can then highlight the Benefits and talk about how you will do it. If this suffices, you may never get into the Features of the thing because you have persuaded them on the Implications and Benefits. However, if they want to drill down further after hearing the Benefits, you can then drop into the Features and talk about all of the nuts and bolts. For example, let's take the first point in the table opposite and move from the question about the Implications into the Benefits and then into the Features.

Persuader:	Through the new change management process we are proposing, you will stand out from others because your success in reducing mistakes, driving productivity and having everyone on the same page will be clearly visible.
Persuadee:	How will we do that? *[Moving from Implication to Benefit]*
Persuader:	It is well known that human processes lead to failures. Especially in change management, so we will reduce and where possible eliminate them.
Persuadee:	How will we do that? *[Moving from Benefit to Feature]*
Persuader:	Well, the proposed process takes a systematic approach to human activities and automates it as much as possible before the solution is rolled out to the staff. We do that by ...

Using the Implication, Benefit, Feature flow, you can be interrupted, side-tracked or whatever else and, while it will not be ideal, you will have already hooked the persuadee into the request and shown them why they should be interested.

Focus on the Implications first, then Benefits, then Features. It is at this point that your preparation and understanding of the persuadee's needs will allow you to increase their receptivity and give them what they need to say 'yes' to your request!

Monitor the persuadee

During this process it is critical that you monitor the persuadee and look for signs that they are becoming excited or disinterested. If you notice they are becoming excited, this tells you that you are on the right track and will allow you to quickly assess where they are in the seven point continuum mentioned in chapter 11 (p. 69).

If the persuadee becomes disinterested, move out of the Features and back into the Implications zone to reengage them. As mentioned earlier, it is important that you do not over- or under-persuade; so, this process is more about the persuadee and identifying their motivation than it is about you presenting all the information you have.

In my former company, we would occasionally be required to meet with a new client to pitch for business. As most of our work came via referral, this was not that common and, therefore, the pitch was reasonably structured and linear in approach. It covered who we were, what we did, who else we worked with and then involved us covering what we thought the prospect needed to know about our products and services before asking if they had any questions.

Around the middle of 2008, we moved to a self-directed pitching model which meant that the pitch was directed by the client. To be able to provide what they wanted to know or when they wanted to know it, we had to have full flexibility in our pitch deck to go to any page, at any time.

While not revolutionary, this enabled us to spend more time up front to confirm our research and identify what their problems actually were. We were then able to draw the Implications for them based on what they had told us and to follow the path they required, which inevitably led to persuading them to use our services because they could see how we were able to deliver their best interests.

We weren't pitching for new business, we were providing them with the opportunity to buy from us.

Implications for you

- Understanding why you are doing something is critical to how you communicate your request. To ascertain this, use the Five Whys technique.

- Communicating your request in such a way that taps into the persuadee's best interests will give you every chance of success. To do this, draw the Implications for the persuadee first, followed by the Benefits and, finally, finish with the Features of the thing only if needs be.

13. Where

When planning your Persuasion Strategy, you need to consider when and where you will deliver your request. This will be influenced by your stakeholder analysis, the PEAK, your Aim and the persuadee's receptivity.

In an interview I recently conducted with Dr Robert B. Cialdini (see p. 125), he made a point that could be easily overlooked due to its simplicity. He said something that he found remarkable when conducting his systematic field-based research (which ultimately led to the discovery of the six universal Principles of Persuasion that we will discuss in chapters 19–25) was that there are really two domains that are available to increase the success of an attempt to persuade someone in your direction. He identified these two domains as:

1. The content of what you are offering.

2. The context or the psychological frame in which the offer or request is placed.

This comment is truly insightful because all too often we focus on the content alone. We look at the features of our product or service. We focus on what we do and create a letter, email, pitch or website based around the content. Yes, the content is important, but if you focus just on what you do, making it overwhelmingly detailed and polished, you can lose the persuadee long before you have the chance to get them to say 'yes' to your request.

The critical aspect, therefore, is the context. It is the psychological frame in which the persuadee considers the content. For example, if you go to see the most marvellous painting but when you arrive it is in a dark corner, housed in an old damaged frame, with larger more commanding pieces surrounding it, it will appear small and unimpressive. The painting will probably fail to live up to your expectations, and rightfully so. The context in which the picture is encountered is all wrong. Take the same piece of art, properly lit, perfectly framed and in a space that allows for its admiration: the context in which the painting is viewed changes our perspective of it. The painting itself is the same, that is, the content is the same. It is the context in which it is considered that is different.

 A frame is one among a number of possible ways of seeing something; reframing is a way of seeing it differently, in effect changing its meaning.[27] Where something is encountered can significantly contribute to how it is seen by the persuadee.

Therefore, in planning to make your persuasive appeal, think about the context in which it can be delivered to show it in its best possible light. Is it in a formal oral presentation, a written brief, an email or a one-on-one conversation?

As Paul Jones notes: 'Sometimes the best email is a phone call.'[28]

Bearing in mind the crucial role that context plays, consider what steps you can take to ensure that your location works with your content in making your argument persuasive. You might consider:

- The room to be used, including the lighting, temperature and even what is on the walls

- The seating

- The medium of delivery

- The supporting materials

- Your level of dress

- Any distractions that may impact on your delivery, such as:
  - Telephones
  - Email
  - Assistants or other staff
  - Upcoming meetings, etc.

Once you have considered these aspects, it is then your job as the persuader to manage them as best as you can so they enhance your request, not detract from it.

Implications for you

- Consider how you are framing your content by where you deliver it.

- Content is important, but it is not the only thing.

14. When

It is said that timing is everything, and this is certainly true in the presentation of your persuasive request. In every interaction we have with others there are multiple opportunities to persuade. These opportunities occur in every interaction, with everyone, every day. Therefore, opportunities need to be planned and prepared for to ensure the opportunity is not wasted.

As mentioned in chapter 9, when conducting your research take note of the times of day and night that your persuadee is online, in the office, in the car or even in meetings (see p. 47). By having an understanding of their schedule, you will be better placed to identify a time that best suits the type of request you are seeking to make. For example, if you need the persuadee to sit, listen and reflect on what is being said, for a leader these opportunities are rare during standard office hours due to the many distractions they face.

 To set up a face-to-face meeting with a time-poor leader, you may call at a time you know they have something to go to, e.g. a management meeting. In your short conversation, acknowledge they are busy, suggest a meeting at an alternate time and ask to lock it in. They are more likely to accept the meeting for the day and time you have suggested than if you had called when they were quiet. Had you done so, instead of taking the in-person meeting, they would have been more likely to say: 'Let's just discuss it over the phone now.'

Crafting an opportunity

Often, being in the right place at the right time is like a game of chance, but it can also come about from an incredibly well-crafted opportunity.

 A mentee of mine, Jill, became involved in a project that her leadership identified was important for the business. One leader, Adrian, who was particularly interested in the project, requested that a proposal be submitted to support a concept that Jill raised in a staff meeting. The proposal was completed and submitted for forwarding up the chain of command as requested. For reasons unknown, Jill's supervisor failed to pass the documents up to the leader as requested, despite gentle reminders and prompts from Jill.

Jill called me for advice on how she should approach this situation because the proposal would be a great opportunity for her career advancement.

I asked her what opportunities existed in her day to interact with Adrian. Due to the reluctance of Jill's supervisor, it would be inappropriate to make a formal approach to Adrian; however, an informal conversation in a hall or a shared elevator would not be.

The opportunity was to be crafted over a cup of tea in the morning, where a provocative statement (a statement that requires a response – not the inappropriate kind) could be made.

The statement was: 'It looks like all of the new projects are getting off the ground quickly.' It would be effective because Jill's proposal related to a new project, and she knew there was a high likelihood that after some conversation about the other projects Adrian would ask a question about the proposal Jill was preparing.

The next day Jill arrived at work early as usual and at the time she knew Adrian was normally in the tea room she walked in with her cup. Without prompting, Adrian said 'Hi Jill. How's that proposal coming along?'

This was a persuasive opportunity, and Jill responded that it had come together really well and had been submitted over a week ago for consideration. Jill offered to email a copy through to Adrian so he could read it before the crowds poured in, as there were a couple of points that were reasonably complex. She emailed the proposal, and it was approved within the hour.

It is all about timing and the careful use of it.

Outside world

When considering a persuasive approach, make sure you keep close tabs on current events. Often, events that are happening in the broader environment may not only have an impact on your request but can be leveraged to maximize or craft a persuasive opportunity. For example, delivery of the annual government budget may be a perfect opportunity to reengage with persuadees to discuss the impact it has on them. Similarly, temporal events like celebrations, festive seasons or seasonal activities may also provide an appropriate avenue for engagement.

 The context of the broader environment and what is happening right now can make your persuadee more or less receptive to your request.

Their world

Just as the broader environment can create opportunities, you also need to be aware of the things that are occurring around the persuadee, such as staffing numbers, deadlines, budgets and even activities occurring outside of work in their family or social groups.

For example, if someone has gone off sick, three staff are away at a conference and the email system has just failed, this is probably not the best time to walk into the boss's office to try to persuade her to let you take a year-long sabbatical to study for your MBA.

REMEMBER THIS!!!

Consider the personal context within which your request will be received. Look at the things that are occurring around your persuadee at this point in time; just because you *can* say something doesn't mean you should.

Be prepared

Spontaneous opportunities appear that you may not be able to craft, but you can be ready if they occur. By considering in advance your Aim and the PEAK, you will become vigilant to any opportunity that arises, thus allowing you to identify the opportunity and seize it.

Often, spontaneous opportunities are perfectly framed because something has just occurred that makes this the right time and place to deliver your request.

Implications for you

• Consider the broader and immediate environments when seeking to make your persuasive request.

• Ensure you focus on the type of opportunity you are seeking so you become vigilant to it.

• Timing is everything. Be prepared.

15. Persuasive opportunities

Seizing opportunities

Opportunities need to be recognized and seized, otherwise they will diminish over time. Therefore, whether an opportunity is crafted or simply appears, it must be identified and maximized based upon your plan.

To seize an opportunity you must:

1. Identify it
2. Apply relevant tools in response
3. Maximize the opportunity
4. Watch out for the next one.

 In every interaction, every day, there are multiple opportunities, circumstances or situations to influence someone else.

A crisis is an opportunity

We have all experienced a crisis of one sort or another. But regardless of the size, a crisis by definition is a crucial stage or turning point in the course of something. Therefore, whether the crisis is real or perceived, it is a great opportunity to persuade others because of the situation it creates – think of a crisis as a trigger for change! Yes, at times it will be a big, hairy, unwanted trigger but a trigger nonetheless.

REMEMBER THIS!!!

A crisis is a trigger for change, not something to be feared! It is a terrible opportunity to waste!

Missing opportunities

It is human nature that you will miss some of the opportunities that present themselves. However, it is important that if you do miss one, you recognize it as a missed opportunity and become vigilant for similar opportunities in the future. More importantly, opportunities should not be ignored because not only will that opportunity be terminated, but over time if too many opportunities are missed or ignored they will stop coming.

THINK ABOUT IT

You are at work one day and a friend calls you all excited. They have had to come downtown and are near your building. They don't get into the city very much and want to catch up for a coffee. You thank them for the offer but decline because you are too busy.

The next week the same friend rings again. They are going to be in the city later that day and again want to know if you are available for a coffee. Again you decline, apologizing that you have a meeting you cannot get out of.

These are both opportunities. Yes, to make the coffee appointment with your friend, but also to set up another time, even on the weekend, that is more convenient for you both.

If, as in this situation, you just say sorry, you are terminating the opportunity. If this continues to happen, over time the opportunities will stop coming; your former friend will not bother calling you anymore because you are always too busy to see them!

Learn from missed opportunities

To ensure you learn from missed opportunities, reflect on the following steps:

1. Identify the missed opportunity
2. Become vigilant to any further opportunities with that person
3. Seize the next opportunity when it comes along
4. Apply the relevant tools
5. Maximize the opportunity
6. Watch out for future opportunities.

Implications for you

- Opportunities can be maximized, missed or lost. Maximize those that you seize and learn from those that are missed or lost.

- Don't miss or ignore persuasive opportunities over and over again and expect people to say 'yes' to your requests.

16. How

It is at this point in the planning phase that the rubber really hits the road. Up until now we have looked at what we want to achieve. This step focuses on how we go about it. Many people want to skip straight to this point. It is critical, however, that the earlier steps are considered, even if only briefly, to ensure you are able to carry out this step successfully.

 You need to know where you want to go before you can work out how you are going to get there.

Link your Aim to your execution

It is important to quickly refer back to your Aim to confirm that what you originally set is achievable now you have considered all of the other factors.

Next you need to break down each of the tasks that will need to be undertaken for you to achieve your Aim. It is important that you don't try to put the tasks into priority order just yet; instead, spend your time articulating what you need to do and then nominate the sequence in which you will execute them.

If it makes it easier, think of your Persuasion Strategy as a cooking recipe. Your Aim is a cake you want to end up with, and the steps you are considering here are the ingredients that need to go into the cake. To get your cake just right, you need to add the right ingredients in the right amounts at the right time.

By way of example, let's return to our challenge with our OD Leader.

Aim	To gain the Organizational Development Leader's support for the delivery of a new change management programme by October, allowing it to commence in the next calendar year
Tasks	1. Ascertain the OD Leader's attitude toward organizational change 2. Ascertain the OD Leader's attitude toward this project 3. Obtain a commitment for this project 4. Obtain a commitment for the time frame 5. Create a project plan 6. Obtain support for executive lobbying in advance of the presentation 7. Conduct executive lobbying with the support of the OD Leader 8. Present to the Executive Development Committee 9. Secure approval and resources

As you can see from this table, each of the tasks contributes to achieving the Aim. You will also note that they start broad and then narrow to the specific tasks. In this circumstance, it is critical to ascertain the leader's attitude toward organizational change before making the link to the current project. Only then can the commitment be secured for the support and timeline, leading to the nuts and bolts being fleshed out in the project plan. With the project plan developed, this allows for the articulation of the lobbying required, and by whom, before progressing to the presentation to the Executive Development Committee.

The critical point to note here is: if the first task is not achieved, it does not mean the rest of the tasks are redundant. Instead, it informs the remainder of the tools and tactics to be employed, the paths to be used, the persuadees to be focused upon and, only then, the ability to progress through the remainder of the strategy.

Consider your strategy options

Throughout the planning process you have identified what you need; who you need to persuade, their attitude toward what you are proposing and why they care; when and where you might engage them; and the tasks that are required to be completed to achieve your Aim.

With all that in mind you are now ready to consider some options, or how you intend to approach your tool selection in order to achieve your Aim. Some examples of strategies that will dictate certain types of tool selection are:

- Building relationships
- Repairing relationships
- Confirming understanding
- Reinforcing positions
- Overcoming uncertainty
- Shaping decisions

- Changing decisions
- Informing/educating
- Instructing
- Requesting action
- Driving action.

The tools and tactics required to support these strategies are covered in section 3.

Identify your persuader

While a controversial point, you may need to consider that the best person to make the pitch, presentation or request may not be you. Identify the right person for each task and remember that they do not have to be the same person.

 Think back to a previous encounter where the entire process fell apart because of the person delivering the message. What would have happened if someone else took the role of primary communicator?

It is important that you match your persuader to your persuadee and to the context within which the presentation will be made.

Refer to the Persuasion Strategy Template at the end of this chapter for a better idea of how best to format these steps to create a cohesive and complete Persuasion Strategy.

Ability to execute

Finally, in executing any Persuasion Strategy, there are a few golden rules you must consider. Start by asking yourself, is what I am asking going to:

1. Take too long?

2. Be too expensive?

3. Demand too much physical effort on the part of the persuadee?

4. Demand too much cognitive effort on the part of the persuadee?

5. Have the persuadee deviate from any existing social norms?

6. Have the persuadee step outside of their normal routine?

If the answer to any of the above is 'yes', then what you are asking is not going to be seen as easy, which will create friction, and friction creates resistance toward you and/or your request.

Implications for you

*   Go back and confirm that your Aim is achievable.

*   Identify the tasks that are required to achieve your Aim.

*   Determine the appropriate tool and persuader for each task.

*   Show the persuadee that what you are asking them to do is easy.

Persuasion Strategy Template

WHAT					
Aim • Specific • Measurable • Active • Realistic • Timely					

WHO					
Persuadee(s) by category	Name	Decision Maker	Indirect Leader	Influencer	Other

Persuasion Map • Colour code • Circle size • Labels • Arrows • Line weight	
Barriers to access	
Identified Persuasion Hubs	
Path(s) to persuadee	
Essentials • Persuadee's priorities	Meaning	
	Security	
	Connections	
	Recognition	
	Action	
	Motivators: • Intrinsic • Extrinsic	

Attitude	Belief – True/False	
	Values – Right/Wrong	
Receptivity	–3 ——— –2 ——— –1 ——— 0 ——— 1 ——— 2 ——— 3 Hostile Indifferent Active	
Knowledge	What do they already know?	
	What don't they know?	
	What do they need to know?	
	What don't they need to know?	

WHY	
Your Reason • Five Whys	
Their Reason • Implication • Benefit • Features	

WHERE	
Context • Location • Medium • Resources • Attire • Distractions	

WHEN	
Opportunities • Known • Crafted • Be ready for • Outside factors • Their world	

HOW			
	Task	Tool/Tactic	Persuader

SECTION 3: Tools

The concept of the carrot and the stick comes from the traditional alternatives of getting a donkey to move by either holding out a carrot, enticing it to move forward, or by punishing it and hitting it with a stick, thus forcing it to move.

When dealing with people, inducements or rewards represent the carrot. They create or drive change by incentivizing the persuadee to do what you want them to.

The stick represents coercion and this is where power or some form of penalty is used to create the desired behaviour.

Inducements promise positive consequences, coercion negative consequences. For our purposes, we want to use tools, framing and content to effect change at a belief level, motivating people into a desired behaviour.

Reactions to persuasion

People generally react to persuasion in three different ways:

- **Commitment**: They agree internally with an action or decision, are enthusiastic about it, and are likely to exercise initiative and demonstrate unusual effort and persistence in order to carry out the request successfully.

- **Compliance**: They carry out the requested action but

are apathetic rather than enthusiastic, make only a minimal or average effort, and do not show any initiative.

- **Resistance**: They oppose the requested action and try to avoid carrying it out by refusing, arguing, delaying, or seeking to have the request nullified.

In this section, we will introduce the tools to engage the persuadee to exercise initiative and persistence, as well as the tools to overcome compliance and reduce resistance, where necessary.

17. Stories

Persuasion comes in many forms: written, oral and blended. It occurs between individuals, groups, organizations and even countries. Whether you want to motivate, organize, shape, engage, win over or do anything else, stories are an effective means of grabbing attention and moving people in your direction.

For centuries, stories have been the vehicle for inspiration, culture and connection. Stories are coded deep within who we are as human beings; they are a means of conveying messages and emotion and of humanizing ourselves to others. People remember and retell stories, and it happens from a young age, as it is accepted that children as young as two can tell and follow stories. As you will know, it is easier to recount and retell a story than it is to recall a series of points from a list.

'But people in business don't tell stories'

I have heard it said that in business there is no place for stories. Business is all about facts, figures, evidence and details. It is not warm and fuzzy. Well, I am here to tell you that is rubbish. Some of the greatest leaders were those who had the ability to tell stories. They created tension and drama, mystery and intrigue, before drawing the audience in and holding them long past the point they thought possible.

Listen to any speech from a great orator: the exceptional storytelling makes the time quickly evaporate.

However, the inverse is also true; we have all been in a presentation, seminar or pitch where the presenter was underprepared, read directly from the slides or was just plain boring. Time drags on. If the storytelling is poor, so is the attention span of the audience, and so will be your ability to persuade people in your direction.

Take Simon Sinek's TED talk, for example (see p. 80). I share it with people because he is such a great storyteller. He allows you to experience the story of Wilbur and Orville Wright in a way that no one ever has and uses Samuel Pierpont Langley as a great point of contrast. He even positions Apple as a mystery and then quickly solves it for you right before your eyes, all the while talking about a successful computer company.

All great business, political and social leaders have told illustrative and intriguing stories. They get your attention with a challenge or a mystery, then they personalize the experience, making it an emotionally-driven exercise. They tell of struggle and of defeating the odds and have you questioning if what they are saying is really possible. Finally, they provide the resolution, the answer and the epiphany and draw the conclusion for you in a memorable way. This all helps you to remember the content of the story and experience its message.

By way of example, my most successful blog posts usually involve the telling of a story: the sharing of a small part of myself or someone else, not for grandeur or ridicule but for a purpose. The story draws readers in and compels them to engage and interact. Below is one such story:

Today we went to the beach for our weekend family walk, and I will admit I was somewhat distracted because of the national aviation dispute that had ground flights to a halt. Thousands of travellers were stranded, and plans were in disarray. The 8am meeting I had booked interstate in the morning was most likely going to have to go ahead without me. Anyway, because of this I was regularly checking my phone and not as present as I could have been as the kids played.

For weeks my son Ryan had been battling to successfully skim rocks, and he was continually asking me to select rocks for him, help him with his throwing and to generally encourage him along. I am not sure if it was because I was not pushing as hard for him to do a good job or if he wanted to get my attention, but today he succeeded. With squeals of delight, first it was two skips, then three and the best of the day was eight skips across the water's surface! This, of course, required him to tease his older sisters based on his newly-found prowess.

My eldest daughter Samara decided she now wanted to know how to skip rocks too. I showed her how to select the right rock, how to hold it, how to pick her timing between the waves and then how to throw it. Due to her need to do everything absolutely perfectly on the first try (not sure where that comes from!) we had some frustration, but ultimately we got to the multiple skipping throws quite quickly and she was extremely pleased with herself.

On our return journey down the beach, I was again checking my phone and I looked up momentarily to find the most perfect skipping rock. I excitedly showed my family and said: 'Watch this, I think it can be a ten skipper for sure.' I waited for the perfect wave break, talking it up all the time, and when it came I let it rip. The rock flew through the air quickly, turned onto the vertical and sliced straight into the water without a single hop, skip or jump. I felt like a real goose.

At that point Samara quietly walked up, put her hand on my back and genuinely said 'Nice rock finding, Dad' before walking on.

I was gobsmacked. I felt a glowing sensation of admiration and pride for my daughter, who had the presence of mind to make such a comment, and pure delight that in my embarrassment she delivered a little praise that immediately made me feel better.

She then turned and asked if I would like to follow her footprints in the sand, something she does to me every weekend, and you know what, I shortened my gate and followed her every step. Why? Because she had done such a lovely thing for me and when you like someone you are more inclined to say 'yes' to them.

Perhaps you can take a lesson from Samara. Rather than jibe, joke or react, genuinely praise someone and see if you can create, maintain or enhance your relationship with them, and they may just follow in your footsteps as a result.[29]

The story is a vehicle for the message. It has a structure and delivers a key point to be remembered.

The structure is:

1. Introduce a challenge or mystery.
2. Personalize the content.
3. Overcome or resolve a problem.
4. Provide the takeaway in a memorable form.

Make your story purposeful

Any story you tell must have a purpose. Having done your preparation (chapter 9) and understood both your and the persuadee's 'why' (chapter 12) will make it infinitely easier to select the right story, rather than just telling any old random story for the sake of it. The key is, the sooner your persuadee identifies with you and realizes you have shared goals or things in common, the sooner they will listen, remember and engage.

Therefore, in selecting the story to tell, consider your persuadee. Tell a story that draws the Implication (chapter 12) to the surface for them and immerses them at the same time. Do this by selecting a story that possesses a mystery or a challenge which is similar to that being faced by the persuadee, or at least one that is easily relatable. Be expressive and create some drama by the way you tell the story, using pauses and intonation for effect, and then bring it home with a clear and relevant resolution.

Hitting the buttons

Think about hitting your persuadee's hot buttons in telling

your story. You want to hook them into something they are interested in and something they can draw relevance from. Turning them off or hitting their cold buttons with irrelevant stories will dampen the impact and can confuse them and/ or have them react against you. This is why preparation and research is so critical to the tools and tactics you employ.

 If you hook your persuadee and they are focusing on what comes next, they pay attention, they listen and they engage. If the story is one that is well-known, overused or irrelevant, it will do the opposite.

It is important to watch your persuadee as you tell them your story. Watch their face for the 'aha moment' when they realize what you have just told them. This is what the storytelling process is all about. In that moment, your persuadee has not just heard your story, they have experienced it, and that is persuasive gold.

Stories and fairy tales
As mentioned in section 1, being unethical and manipulating others are sure-fire ways to destroy your reputation. Therefore, when telling stories, if you are claiming something happened to you, make sure it did. In today's interconnected world, it is too easy to check the accuracy of a story and what happened to whom. While stories engage

and have the power to pull persuadees in, they can also be a reputation killer if you are found to be making things up. If you want to embellish and step beyond the facts of what really happened, set it up as a hypothetical rather than a personal story.

Putting it into writing

Stories can be conveyed in writing, but they must be clear, purposeful and not too long. For example, narratives in company profiles or on 'about us' pages on websites can disengage readers because they are too long, hard to read and often are more about the persuader than connecting with the persuadee.

Think about the stories you share with colleagues, family and friends. Rarely are they long, formal stories or heavily-edited versions crafted by a copywriter. Instead, they are short, personalized and have a purpose.

Wherever possible, tell stories in person because it allows for authenticity to shine through. If that is not possible, think about the ways you can persuade by using a written story to illustrate your point.

Presenting it

Storytelling is best delivered in person because of the human-to-human (H2H) interaction. After all, persuasion is an H2H activity. The use of tone more accurately communicates meaning, intensity and genuineness. Similarly, stories make facts and figures come to life. They more easily create drama, trigger empathy and allow for the realization to be experienced, not just read. This is probably the reason why many cultures relied on storytelling to pass on their heritage, rather than verbose written texts. Stories connect people, generations and communities.

Even when telling a story over the phone, don't limit your expression by sitting down. Stand up. Open your chest and tell the story as if the person were right in front of you. It will show in your tone and how the story is received.

 Wherever possible, strive to tell your most compelling and engaging stories in person, rather than printing them on a brochure. This is what Steve Jobs was able to do each year when he announced Apple's latest product updates. There was always a story, a journey and 'one more thing', where Jobs would appear to finish, turn as if to walk off the stage, then turn back and proceed to deliver the latest news, new product or insight. He had people hooked, and Apple's share price reacted accordingly.

Using it online

Stories allow for relationships to form. Therefore, when communicating stories over digital media such as websites, videos and so on, think about the relationship you want to build with your audience. A generic video on the home page of your website may be a great humanizing tool, but it may not be the best storytelling platform. Instead, consider the use of webinars, video conferences and hangouts to convey your stories in a more customized and meaningful manner.

The use of audio and video replies to emails is quickly replacing the long-winded written message because it is faster, but also because it allows you to be heard and seen, and this is the perfect platform for storytelling.

Beware

Stories are impactful, and those who would use persuasion against you know this. Be wary of the stories you are told, especially those that appear to be overly emotive and closely reflect your situation. Often, scams involve an elaborate story to draw you in. They talk about the struggle being faced. They personalize it. Then they tell you how the challenge can be overcome with some assistance from you. They often possess the necessary elements of a persuasive story, but their intent is not to help you realize a point or move you in a positive direction. Instead, these stories are used to disarm, using a peripheral route of persuasion to bypass the rational processing centres of the brain. Therefore, to protect yourself ask questions, do research and don't rush in.

Think about things that have happened in your life that you can share with others to move them in your direction. What adversity have

you faced? What successes have you had? If you are struggling to think of a personal story, see if you can weave
others' stories into your presentations to highlight your
point, just as Sinek did with the Wright brothers.

Implications for you

- Embrace storytelling.

- Ensure you reflect on your preparation when selecting
the right story to tell.

- Tell relevant and interesting stories, and look for that
'aha moment' where the persuadee has connected with
you and your message.

- Consider the medium and how best you can convey
your story.

- Avoid commonly used stories.

- Pick the purpose for each story and use it selectively.

- Turn up to meetings early and be available to hang back
late; use this time to set up the meeting or draw implications outside of the formal structured environment by
telling stories.

- Be careful of those who would use storytelling against
you.

18. I, you, we

In persuading people, you need to ensure you adhere to some basic linguistic structures to be successful. For example, when introducing people into a story, you need to explain who the person is ('the actor') and then talk about what they are doing, will do or have done ('the action'). The actor should always precede the action.

One of the most common mistakes I see people make is to talk about themselves before they speak about the persuadee.

Move 'I' to 'you'

It is a simple enough mistake to make. After all, our favourite topic of conversation is usually ourselves. As we saw in chapter 12, you need to draw the Implication for the persuadee and show them what's in it for them. It is very difficult to be persuadee-centric if you start every sentence with 'I' or use too many 'me' words (such as I, me, my, us or our). Instead, use more 'you' words (such as you, your, yourself or their name).

For example, rather than say 'I have attached the document for you', change it to 'You will find the document attached'. It is simpler and now focuses on the persuadee.

By making your text persuadee-centric, more people will read what you are writing and take action accordingly.

Please don't think I am saying take yourself out of the

text altogether. Firstly, it is nearly impossible to achieve. Secondly, there needs to be a minimum of two people involved in any communication, and removing one person will make it read terribly and appear sterile and devoid of personal commitment.

The basic ratio you want to achieve is two mentions of the persuadee to every one reference to yourself. If you can achieve a 3:1 ratio, that is even better.

Go into your sent email folder and select a message that you have sent to someone where you were seeking to move them in your direction.

Copy the text into a word-processing document and count the number of 'you' words versus the number of 'me' words.

If your ratio is not at least 2:1, have a go at reworking some of sentences and putting the persuadee first – especially in the opening sentence.

A brief word of warning. In both written and oral situations, watch your use of tone when using 'you' words to make sure it is not interpreted as accusatory. Too many uses of 'you should' and 'you asked' can alienate your persuadee, as you are speaking *at* them not *to* them.

We

The use of the word 'we' is a little controversial. In a communications sense, 'we' is seen to be a 'me' word and should therefore be avoided. However, 'we' is one of the most important words you can use because it is the quickest and easiest way to describe a relationship. Therefore, I am telling you to use 'we', but use it appropriately.

The proper use of 'we' shows togetherness. It highlights how important the relationship is to you and demonstrates that you are thinking of the persuadee as a partner. For example: 'It is great that we have been open to the use of new technologies.' Here, 'we' celebrates the collective openness.

'We' can also refer to a group of people, for example: 'We think this is a great initiative.' For 'we', a pronoun, to be used in this sense, the noun must already have been introduced (e.g. the actors' names) for it to make sense. If you do not know who 'we' is, that should be your next question.

The use of the 'royal we' – for example, when a monarch or ruler says 'We are not amused' – should be avoided unless you own your own castle. The use of 'we' in this context assumes a greater acceptance on behalf of the business or the team; however, it depersonalizes the interaction and takes it from H2H communication to something altogether different because the members of the 'we' are not known. In this circumstance, identify the 'we'. For example, 'our team believes' or 'my organization holds the view'. This is important because people live within the team and the organization, so identify them and include them in the relationship.

'We' is the fastest and easiest way to communicate a relationship. The word 'with' indicates distance and a separation between the parties.

Therefore, wherever possible, say 'We did this' rather than 'I did this with Bill'.

Putting it into writing

When writing any text, in particular emails, a useful strategy is to get your ideas or message down first and then go back to review it. Pay particular attention to the first line of the email. This is where your Implication should be drawn, and the wording must be persuadee-centric. Ensure you lead with the persuadee, then yourself.

The reason this is particularly effective in emails is because emails are from you to another person or group of people. They are H2H communication and a place where relationships already exist or are being built.

In the body of the text, think about the core elements and where relationships need to be drawn to the surface to demonstrate that you and the persuadee are working together. It is in these key parts that the word 'we' should feature.

Be careful of using 'we' in 'All Staff' or large group emails. In this context, 'we' could easily become a 'me' word and, therefore, make it all about you.

The green light

When receiving emails from Decision Makers, Indirect Leaders and Influencers, be on the lookout for their use of 'we'. Used at appropriate times in the email, it can give you an insight into their thinking. For example,

> Hi Anthony,
>
> Thank you for your time today and for giving our executive group the benefit of your insight into the field of persuasion and how it applies to our business.
>
> As discussed, the next step will be important for our company and our longer-term strategic goals. I believe **we** will be able to develop an industry-leading programme that our people will really benefit from.
>
> Kind regards,
> Andrea

In the above excerpt, 'we' indicates that Andrea is already thinking about the working relationship with Anthony: a small but positive indicator that could be easily missed if you only scan emails.

Review some of your recent email correspondence from a persuadee. Search for the word 'we' and see if you can find the first time it was used. This may indicate the time they consciously moved in your direction.

Presenting it

When delivering a presentation, holding a meeting and even in everyday conversations, think about the ratio of 'you' to 'me' words. Just like our email example, start by talking about the persuadee, not yourself. Make your words persuadee-centric and clearly bring the Implication to the surface for them. At the appropriate time, introduce 'we' into the conversation to demonstrate the forming or existence of the relationship. Of course, don't be too eager to introduce the 'we' if your relationship has not developed to that point yet.

When talking with persuadees, listen to their language and their use of the word 'we'. As we have seen, used at the appropriate time, a persuadee can tell you that you they are already thinking of you as a partner by how they use of the word 'we'.

Similarly, listen carefully to how your persuadee uses 'we' in relation to others. They may just tell you, without really telling you, that they are already working with someone else.

Using it online

In your website copy and marketing materials, especially those focused on the broader audience, ensure your language, offerings and content are persuadee-centric. You may need to draw several Implications to the surface so they can see how what you are offering will make a positive impact on them and their business.

The use of the word 'we' in this context will almost certainly be a 'me' word because no relationship exists up until that point, so consider avoiding it in generic documentation, copy and videos.

Beware

Since Dale Carnegie (p. 12), people have understood that someone's name is the sweetest and, possibly, most important word in any language.[30] Some may seek to use this against you, drawing you in through the use of 'you' words, using your name continuously, introducing 'we' and focusing on the newly-formed relationship. Your task is to assess the genuineness of this approach and see it for what it is: whether a carefully constructed tactic to move you in their direction or a genuine expression of interest and recognition of the working relationship that exists.

Implications for you

- Always make it about the persuadee.

- Refer to them and their needs before yourself and what you want.

- Get your ideas down on paper first and then go back and review the 'you' to 'me' ratio, ensuring it is at least 2:1, preferably 3:1.

- Look for the use of the word 'we' by your persuadee and other stakeholders to gauge the relationship.

- Watch your use of 'you' words to ensure they do not imply accusation.

- Monitor the overuse of your name or the pronoun 'we' by others to assess their genuineness in attempting to persuade you.

19. Cialdini's Principles of Persuasion

The most widely cited and credible persuasion tools in business today are those attributed to the research of Dr Robert B. Cialdini, Regents' Professor at Arizona State University and President of Influence at Work.[31]

Dr Cialdini has spent his career researching the science of persuasion, earning him an international reputation as the 'Godfather of Influence'. His research, publications and ethical business and policy applications cover the fields of persuasion, compliance and negotiation.

What sets Cialdini apart from other social scientists is that he systematically identified and tested compliance strategies he observed in the real world. He interviewed, trained with and learned from practitioners whose job it was to get others to say 'yes' to their requests.

Cialdini relied on two main sources for his conclusions: observing compliance professionals in their normal surroundings and then conducting laboratory experiments to validate his observations. He observed numerous tactics that led to positive responses, but the majority were able to be collated into his six universal Principles of Persuasion, which are outlined in this table:

Cialdini's Principles of Persuasion

Reciprocity	People are inclined to give back to those who have given to them first.
Scarcity	Things appear more valuable if they are rare or dwindling in availability.
Authority	We look to those who have superior knowledge or wisdom on a subject to guide our decisions.
Commitment & Consistency	People tend to remain consistent with the commitments they make.
Liking	We prefer to say 'yes' to those we know and like.
Consensus/ Social Proof	When we are not sure of what we should do, we look to the behaviour of others to guide our decisions.

It is not my intent to simply restate Cialdini's research here; for that you should read his book *Influence*.[32] Instead, the following chapters (20–25) will guide you through the application of the principles.

 Dr Cialdini's animated video, narrated by himself and Steve Martin, is a great introduction to the principles: http://youtu.be/cFdCzN7R Ybw?list=UU8IMseLCZx2BZe3thxHXnog

20. Reciprocity

Reciprocity allows people to build relationships, businesses to thrive and communities to prosper. Reciprocity dictates that people are more willing to comply with requests, return favours, provide services, share information and make concessions to those who have given to them first. I am sure you have felt the pull of obligation when someone has given you a gift or done something special for you, to repay the gesture in kind. This is the pull of Reciprocity, and every society on earth is bound by it.

Numerous research studies have been conducted on Reciprocity, exploring where something is given:

- With the expectation of receiving something in return.

- As an investment in the future with no expectation of return in the short term.

- Simply for the benefit of others with no expectation of return at all.

Gifts

A study called 'Sweetening the till'[33] looked at the effect of servers in restaurants giving their diners an unexpected gift of chocolate when delivering the bill. The researchers looked at what happened if no chocolate was given to establish a baseline. They then looked at the impact when one chocolate was given to each diner on the tray with the bill: the server was able to increase their tips by 3.3 per cent. If the server gave two chocolates to each diner, the tip rose by 14.1 per cent over the no chocolate condition. The final condition saw the server first give one piece of chocolate. They then turned to leave before turning back and giving each diner an extra piece of chocolate (the 1+1 condition). In this instance, the server was able to increase their tip by 23 per cent.

Cialdini, in his collaboration with Steve Martin and Noah Goldstein, *Yes!: 50 Scientifically Proven Ways to Be Persuasive*,[34] highlighted that in the 1+1 condition, three factors increased the potency of the gift: it was significant, personalized and unexpected.

Preparation is the key to giving gifts, in that you need to understand what is important to the persuadee and their current situation, and you need to ensure the things you give – such as opportunities, referrals or information – are significant, personalized to and unexpected by them.

The 'Door in the Face' technique

The second aspect of Cialdini's research on Reciprocity is what he calls the 'request and retreat' strategy or 'Door in the Face' technique. In this instance, the persuader makes an extreme initial request of the persuadee, anticipating that they will say 'no'. Once they do (they slam the door in the persuader's face), the persuader steps back from their initial position to something more reasonable, thereby making a concession. Research has shown the persuadee is then also more likely to make a concession and move toward the persuader's request.

For example, I ask you if I can borrow three of your six staff for a four-week joint project. You say 'no'. I concede and say: 'If that won't work, what about just one staff member for two weeks?' Because I have made the request and retreated, that is, I have made a concession, it is now right that you should consider doing the same and concede to my request.

 It is important to realize that making a concession is not offering a discount up front. It requires the initial request to be made, the rejection to occur, then a concession or subsequent lesser request to be made.

If you have ever watched a television show where two parties are bargaining over a second-hand item, the buyer will often make a concession on the first item to 'break the ice'. They will make an offer, only to be declined, and then will make a concession in order to build a relationship and start the negotiation process moving forward to benefit future purchases. Note that it is better to make a concession on something small, rather than having to do it over something you really need.

Go into every negotiation prepared with two outcomes:

1. What you want
2. What you will take.

In negotiation theory this is commonly referred to as your BATNA: Best Alternative To a Negotiated Agreement.

Setting your BATNA allows you to retreat from your initial request if necessary to start a working relationship where none existed before.

There is, of course, no guarantee that your efforts will always be reciprocated, but when delivered skilfully you are far more likely to receive something in return than if you do not. Like begets like, such as:

- If you give respect, you get respect.

- If you give disrespect, you get disrespect.

- If you do not give ground, you will not be given ground.

Therefore, give that which you wish to receive and give it *first*! If you want extra information, give information first. If you want access to someone's network, then give access to your network first. But remember, only ever giving to immediately get something in return is the least successful form of Reciprocity. Instead, if you give and invest in others with the expectation that over time the relationship will build and they will return the investment in you, then you will succeed. The most genuine form of giving is when you give with no expectation of return at all, instead you continually invest in others.[35]

Intent

The triggering of Reciprocity is linked to the intent behind the gift-giving and the perception of the intent by the recipient.

If something is seen as a *gift*, it is likely to trigger reciprocation. If it is seen as a *reward*, people will work hard to achieve it as long as they feel they can; if they can't, then they may stop trying because the transaction cannot be fulfilled.

If perks of a job are given to staff as a *bribe* to buy compliance, in harder financial times this will be difficult to maintain and performance will waiver as a result. It is also worth noting that bribes may also have deeper implications. If staff perceive that bribes are an appropriate tactic to get things done, it can create an unethical culture where bribery is used by staff because 'that's how we do business around here'.

Finally, if you want to test if your staff see perks of the job as an entitlement, take them away. If the staff get angry, they see the perks as a 'right' of working at the business rather than something that is given to them.

Therefore, be clear about your intent for giving. If you have free water in a waiting area, don't put the refrigerator in clear view where people can just help themselves. Have the water behind the counter and, as people come into the office, make reference to it being a warm day outside and offer them a cool drink as a gift from the company. If the water is easily accessible in the waiting area, it may be seen as an entitlement in doing business with you and, therefore, less valuable.

You must show the effort and resources that go into giving so your gift can be appropriately valued. Let people know you are thinking about them and are providing the gift as a result of their situation. Give with no expectation of return and watch your relationship build as a result.

Putting it into writing

One example of Reciprocity in written form is Randy Garner's 'Post-it Note Persuasion' research.[36] Garner found that when he sent out a survey with a handwritten sticky note placed on the cover letter requesting completion of the survey, more than 75 per cent of the recipients completed it. This compared with 48 per cent of those who received a handwritten instruction on the letter itself and just 36 per cent of the control group who received the survey and letter with no personalized message.

Because of the extra effort and personalized approach, recipients were more likely to reciprocate the effort and complete the survey in return.

CASE STUDY

Brian Ahearn, a friend, fellow CMCT and colleague, used this research when his company mistakenly overpaid commissions to 150 insurance agencies to the tune of $700,000USD. By employing the science of persuasion and placing handwritten sticky notes on each letter sent out, 130 of the 150 agencies returned the money within two weeks and 147 returned the money within two months.

So, it pays to understand the science of persuasion.

See: http://influence-people-brian.blogspot.com/2012/01/700000-great-reasons-to-use-yellow.html

Presenting it

Providing requests orally certainly makes it easier to leverage the 'Door in the Face' technique, allowing you to react instantaneously to the 'no', thereby triggering the concession. It also allows you to read your persuadee and help them recognize that what you are giving them is truly personalized, significant and unexpected.

You can try this anywhere. If you walk down the hallway looking down, the chances of people saying 'hello' are minimal. If, however, you look up and say 'hello' first, the chances of others saying 'hello' back are almost guaranteed. Never hesitate to be first to give in an interaction with others, because it allows for a relationship to build where none had existed before.

Using it online

You will have heard it said that if you give something away on your website, you will build relationships with your visitors. As we saw earlier, however, for Reciprocity to have its greatest impact, the things you are giving (such as ebooks, white papers, videos, etc.) must be relevant to the visitor, something they need and something of value. This may mean you need to segment your market and make multiple things available to suit different visitors, but it is this extra effort that will pay dividends in the long run.

 Not all gifts are the same. Tailor your gift-giving specifically to suit your persuadee. If you are not sure of what to give them – ask!

Beware

Reciprocity scammers

There are, of course, those who will attempt to exploit Reciprocity for their own gain, providing you with a gift or concession hoping to trigger a positive response from you. Marcel Mauss believed we as humans are obliged to receive and, hence, are open to exploitation.[37]

Make sure when accepting gifts, even the intangible, that you are not becoming indebted to the giver by accepting a seemingly small gift that may lead to a larger request later.

Furthermore, using the 'Door in the Face' technique, a

scammer will make an over-inflated initial offer, retreating to a 'lower' price that is probably the normal, full price of the item, and they get you to pay it by manipulating you with Reciprocity.

Non-reciprocators

Those who do not live by the rule of Reciprocity will happily take from you while not reciprocating themselves. If this is the case, see them for what they are and stop giving.

In the workplace, we often see people bend over backwards to assist others by always doing things for them. If this assistance is not reciprocated and the staff member becomes overloaded, a leader needs to recognize this exploitation and step in to stop it. It will eventually have a detrimental impact on the giver's self-esteem and personal productivity and, from an interpersonal perspective, will make them feel they cannot say 'no' because it has become expected of them and they don't want to let anyone down.

Reciprocal opportunities

When giving to others, ensure there are equal opportunities for them to return the favour, gift or service to you. If you are locked down in meetings or have a closed door policy, it is difficult for others to re-invest in you and your relationship. Therefore, if you give to others, you also have to allow opportunities to occur for them to give back to you. Don't be too quick to judge someone as a non-reciprocator if you are not allowing them an opportunity to reciprocate.

TRY IT NOW! Think about a persuadee with whom you need to build, repair or maintain a relationship. What can you give them – your time, some extra effort, a referral – purely to invest in the relationship? Perhaps a phone call just to catch up would be sufficient.

Implications for you

- Allow your persuadee to see the effort you have made in making the request customized, personalized and unexpected.

- Like begets like. If you are negative toward others, this is what you will get in return.

- Be the first to give. Never be afraid of non-reciprocation because Scarcity (see the next chapter) will protect you.

- Not all gifts are the same. Tailor them to your persuadee.

- Give your time, advice or expertise to those who truly need and value it.

- Don't give to everyone all of the time; value yourself and what you have to offer.

- Invest in others and provide opportunities for them to return the investment.

- Never fear 'no'. Enter every situation with a back-up

option, especially when you anticipate possible rejection. Leveraging the 'Door in your Face' will allow a negotiation to progress rather than stall.

- Beware the gifts you accept from others and the intent behind them.

- Beware an over-inflated first request quickly followed by a concession designed to have you automatically say 'yes'. Recognizing this tactic empowers you to say 'no'.

21. Scarcity

While every culture on Earth teaches Reciprocity, every organism is driven by Scarcity. Quite simply, if you do not have enough to live, you die. It is this fundamental extrinsic motivator that drives behaviour.

Scarcity-based calls to action are everywhere, every day, such as 'for a limited time only', 'only two left in stock' or 'get yours before they are all gone'. They are based on the fact that people are motivated to act when things are rare or dwindling in availability.

CASE STUDY

One story that is perhaps a myth, perhaps not, is that of King Frederick II, the third king of Prussia, and the humble potato.

King Frederick recognized the potato was a potentially lifesaving food source that could sustain his subjects. He valued the return on investment it gave: requiring only a small plot of land, it would feed many.

This is where the myth of the Potato King comes in. It is said that the people did not want to plant nor eat potatoes. So what was he to do? The legend goes that Frederick ordered that the potato be declared the food of the king: not fit for common consumption. He ordered that his potato field be guarded and that commoners be restricted from accessing its royal bounty.

This obvious use of the Scarcity principle piqued the attention of the population and increased their desire for this wondrous new 'royal food'.

In a masterstroke, King Frederick ordered his guards to be less than diligent at night to let the crop be stolen by the villagers so they could plant it in their own gardens. And steal, plant and eat the potato they did!

With this unique approach, Frederick the Potato King was successful in bringing a much needed resource to his country, all through the clever use of Scarcity.

Taking a lesson from the Potato King: value the product you have and others will want it too. Here are some practical tips to get others to value what you have:

- Tell your staff that a new project is opening up and participation will be strictly by invitation only.

- Tell the participants of a meeting at the outset that you will be collecting the briefing papers before they leave the room for confidentiality reasons, thereby placing a high value on the information in the meeting. Watch their attention and interest in the documents rise to new levels.

- Put the book your children won't read on the top shelf and tell them they are not old enough to read it.

The bookends of persuasion

Anything you give in Reciprocity can be restricted in Scarcity; remember, things are more valuable when they are less available.

In the Reciprocity chapter we saw the need to ensure what you give to others is of value to them. Therefore, if your resources are not being valued or are becoming expected, restricting access to them will drive their value back up. Similarly, if someone is happy to receive but not to repay, stop giving.

Loss

Another key element of Scarcity discovered by Cialdini is that people are more motivated by what they stand to lose than what they stand to gain.

For example, one day when I went to my mailbox I found a brochure that was professionally presented on heavyweight green paper and folded into quarters.

On the front page it had two statements in large black font:

Attention Sunshine Coast Regional Council Residents. Will you miss out on the biggest Federal Government hand-out this year?

The obvious Scarcity saw me flip it straight over. On the back cover it had a Scarcity double-play:

Shrinks 12am midnight 30th June.

The statements on this piece of paper clearly showed me I could be missing out on something and I had a deadline (limited time does not have the same impact as limited number, but it is useful all the same), so I was motivated to open up the brochure and read on.

I then saw another statement in bold black text, this time on a white background:

You stand to lose up to $5,000 in solar hand-outs if your new system is not installed by midnight 30th June.

This was a Scarcity triple-play and I wasn't even into the advertisement yet!

At this stage I stopped reading as a consumer because I had installed a solar system on my house eighteen months prior, so I didn't stand to lose anything; however, it did validate my earlier purchase decision and comforted me in the knowledge I wasn't missing out on anything. As a persuasion strategist, I admired the tradecraft in this simple brochure because the provider of this advertisement had got me to do something the others had not – I opened it and read it before I had walked off my driveway.

Critically, in the body of the copy, the company provided clear steps of how I could easily avoid the loss by acting now.

REMEMBER THIS!!! If your loss-framed message could potentially scare people and induce fear, you must provide them with the clear steps of how to avoid the loss. If you do not provide the steps in an easy-to-follow format, the 'freeze-fight-flight' response could see them do nothing, run away and hide or start fighting to protect themselves, thereby reacting against you, not moving toward you.

The worst kind of loss

We have all experienced a situation where we did not take action when we had the opportunity. For example, you see a rare item in a shop and have the opportunity to buy it, but you walk away, only to return later to find it gone. At that moment, you feel the associated regret linked with your inaction.

Similarly, you have probably felt the regret associated with a decision you have made but got wrong; for example, you fixed a home loan interest rate during a period of increasing uncertainty, only to see the interest rates fall considerably over the following months, leaving you paying the higher rate.

A study by Gilovich and Medvec found that 75 per cent of participants polled said they experienced greater regret for the things in life *they did not do* over the regrettable actions they *did do*.[38]

Another study by Kinnier and Metha found that, when asked if they could live their life over to do something differently, people of varying ages (between 20–64 years) were more likely to say they would rectify some regrettable inaction rather than a regrettable action.[39] However, when asked what their biggest regret of the past week was, they were more likely to report things they had done, i.e. a regrettable action. An explanation for this is that when focusing on the present, we are still in damage control mode, looking for ways to rectify a regrettable action. In the short term, regrettable actions can be remedied. Whereas with missed opportunities or regrettable inaction, the opportunity is fleeting and difficult to recapture and, therefore, there may never be an opportunity for a second chance.

Practically then, if you are considering an action but fear the consequences, consider how difficult it will be to reclaim ground through apologies and subsequent action if it goes wrong, i.e. recovering from a regrettable action. You will have an emotional event such as anger or embarrassment, but this will fade with time. Then consider the consequences if you fail to act at all and the chances of this opportunity ever coming around again, i.e. the impact of regrettable inaction. You are far more likely to experience despair and other associated emotions that are likely to last a lifetime. Therefore, any action is often better than no action at all. The caveat here, of course, is always consider the risk and your personal circumstances.

For a practical example of both regrettable action and inaction see Kamil Krolak's '50 People One Question' (http://youtu.be/LP7pdAn3foE). The question is: 'What is your greatest regret?'

Competition

Where the persuadee is genuinely in competition with others for your resources, especially time, let them know your resources are limited and in demand.

It is also worthwhile to occasionally say 'no' to requests for your time or services to highlight that you are busy and people can't get to you anytime they feel like it. This shows that what you have to offer is valuable and other people want it.

Highlighting competition will also ensure that when you have a spot open up in your calendar, people will jump at the chance to book it before someone else does.

What happens when Scarcity fails to drive behaviour?

Recently I had a client come to me and say: 'I have tried to use Scarcity by highlighting that the person is in competition with someone else. When I tell them about the competition they say: "That's okay, go with the other person."'

In one fell swoop the competition evaporated, for both parties. My client wanted to know why people shrug off the competition and say 'no thanks'.

The reason they brush it off is because Scarcity has been brought in too early!

Before you introduce Scarcity, you need to have an understanding of what the persuadee's motivation is. You need to understand if they want to do the thing you are asking or if they are indifferent toward the request.

The key is to ask questions first. Obtain commitments from the persuadee (see chapter 23). Make sure the thing being proposed is of interest to them. Once they have committed, use Consensus (see chapter 25) to show them what people just like them are doing in similar circumstances and then – and only then – highlight that they are in competition with others for the product, commodity or opportunity.

That way, they know what you are offering is of value and, by highlighting the competition, dwindling in availability, which will motivate the persuadee to take action.

If your persuadee can take or leave it, highlighting competition too early will be a hit or miss proposition.

Putting it into writing

When using Scarcity in written form, clearly show what you bring to the table. Draw the Implication, highlight your truly unique Features and show that your product or service is the only one that can offer this combination or service.

In a heavily-crowded commercial space, sometimes your competitive advantage is your staff rather than the product, so bring this to the surface. Show the persuadee what they stand to lose (your team), not what they stand to gain.

If you only ever compete on price, you will be restricted to discounting and giveaways as a means of using Scarcity. By drawing the Implication and unique Features, you are now able use Scarcity to its fullest potential and thus compete on value.

Presenting it

In presenting face to face, honestly highlight the limited

time and capacity you have available. Discuss the others you are working with and the demands this will put on your time. Ask questions, have the persuadee nominate what is important to them and show them that if they do not take the recommended path, they may not be able to have what they want or it may be more expensive if they do not act before a certain time.

Be sure to set a deadline and stick to it. For a deadline to be meaningful, if they miss it they must miss out. This ensures they won't miss it again. If you provide a deadline but always let it slip, any future deadlines will be disregarded because you don't really mean it!

Using it online

Scarce is best but only if you tell others about it. Use countdown timers and even limit the release or availability of stock to keep demand high. Online auctions, such as on eBay, are built on Scarcity: the ability for bidders to see the item, the competition they face and the looming deadline. This in and of itself may be enough to see bidders pay over what they had originally been prepared to. Consequently, if potential buyers miss out on an item, they will bid stronger and earlier on the next auction so as not to miss out again, thereby mitigating the loss.

Scarcity scammers

We have all heard stories of Scarcity being falsely employed when buying something. Imagine you are in an electronics store admiring a product you have long wanted. Even at its sale price it is expensive. Upon saying you need to talk to your partner about it, the sales assistant announces they only have one left in stock and, with the number of people who have looked at it today, they don't expect it to be here by the close of business. The thought of losing out to a rival frequently turns a fence sitter into a buyer, regardless of whether the competition is real or not.

If the competitor is genuine, then so be it. If the rival has been fabricated to move you from fence sitting into buying, it's a scam. Why? Because it is not true. The sales person has introduced information that does not genuinely exist. While it is a win for them, it may not be a win for you, as you were duped into the purchase.

Scarcity is one of the most commonly used tactics because it is relatively easy to introduce and hard to disprove. If you do suspect a scam, don't be afraid to walk away.

Have a look at your website, your last proposal or email, and review your use of Scarcity. Have you highlighted:

- What your persuadee stands to lose?
- A limited number?
- A limited time?
- Any existing complications?

If not, how could you have highlighted this honestly to ensure your persuadee was motivated to take action?

Implications for you

- Scarcity is an extrinsic motivator: it uses external factors to drive behaviour.

- People are motivated by what they stand to lose.

- Restrict your resources when they are not being valued.

- If you give to others and they do not reciprocate, restrict access to the things you have been giving until they come to value them.

- Say 'no' occasionally to highlight that you are not always available.

- If you only have a limited number of resources available, tell people.

- If people are in competition for your resources, tell them.

- If something is only available for a period of time, tell people and stick to the deadline.

- If you will be unavailable for a period of time, contact your persuadees to tell them, but indicate you have time now to finalize things for them.

- Allow them an opportunity to use your services and bring Scarcity to the surface to motivate them to act.

22. Authority

When we are not sure of what we should do, we look to recognized authorities to guide our behaviour. This is because people are more willing to follow the direction or recommendations of someone to whom they attribute superior knowledge and wisdom on a particular matter.

A classic example is Camel's 1949 advertisement, 'More Doctors Smoke Camels Than Any Other Cigarette'.[40] In the ad, Camel showed doctors smoking their brand to leverage the Authority position of the doctor and to encourage consumers to smoke this brand of cigarette over others.

What would be the reaction today if a cigarette company attempted to use medical professionals to promote its products? I think uproar would just about cover it.

The impartiality of professionals such as doctors and dentists is critical to society, and that is why their endorsements are so highly valued. It is also the reason why actors who play doctors are used to promote products, in an attempt by the advertiser to make an authoritative link.

Cues that persuade

Authority in and of itself is not persuasion. It is the cues of Authority that do the persuading.

For example, in 2007 the *Washington Post* conducted an experiment with world-class violinist Joshua Bell. Bell went to a Metro station wearing jeans, a T-shirt and a baseball cap. He had his $3.5 million Stradivarius violin, and for 45 minutes he played six masterpieces. Bell normally filled concert halls, but on this January morning 1,097 people passed his performance: 27 gave money totalling $32.17 (less than one third of the ticket price to see Bell in concert); seven people stopped for at least a minute; and 1,070 people rushed by without as much as a glance.[41]

If Bell were in a concert hall, in a suit, and advertised a free 45-minute concert featuring six classic pieces to be played on his $3.5 million Stradivarius, he would have got a very different response. Why? Not because Bell had extra expertise in the concert hall over what he had in the subway, but because of the cues or trappings that convey this expertise (in the concert hall he is a master, in the station he is a mere busker).

If you are striving to establish your Authority, you need to be seen as *an* Authority (someone with extra knowledge or wisdom).

This is not to be mistaken for someone who is *in* Authority (i.e. the boss).

A boss is able to use incentives and penalties to achieve their goals. An Authority is someone who commands attention when they speak or act because of who they are, what they do and what they know. Therefore, think about the trappings of Authority and what the persuadee is looking for in order to assess your level of expertise and whether you have more knowledge or wisdom than they do in relation to a particular topic. This may be conveyed by such cues as:

- Your dress

- Your business card

- Your title

- Your qualifications

- Your resources (e.g. laptop, tablets, type of phone, quality of pen, type of violin)

- The location of or the fact that you have an office

- The look, feel and functionality of your website

- Current membership or office bearer roles in industry associations

- Peer reviews

- Publications

- The quality of the tools you use.

Expertise

Authority is a critical factor when the persuadee has no other basis by which to assess your expertise, so don't hide these cues away where no one can find them. Often, the persuadee is most uncertain of your expertise during the first meeting or interaction with you. This is where you should highlight your expertise by:

- Providing links in introductory emails to your professional profile or qualifications listed on an 'about us' page on your company website.

- Showing your qualifications and awards in an email signature block.

- Sending a letter of introduction in advance of a meeting highlighting who will be present, their specific areas of expertise and the projects they have been involved in.

- Displaying degrees and diplomas on the wall of your waiting area.

- Forwarding a list of publications you have written.

Remember, the point of the above is not to brag about how good you are. The purpose is to convey to your persuadee that you have high-level knowledge and skills. If you do not bring your prowess to the surface, they will not be able to defer to you as an Authority because they will not know you are one.

TRY IT NOW!

Have a look at your email signature block, LinkedIn profile and any other online profiles you have. Do they truly demonstrate your expertise to those who do not know you?

It is always preferable to establish your Authority in advance of a request being made. However, if the opportunity to establish your credentials in advance is not practicable, there are a few things you can do when it comes time to meet.

Show your knowing

To move people in your direction, you need show them that you know your stuff. You do not need to name drop, but you do need to demonstrate you are up with industry developments and relevant international trends and that you participate in activities to advance your industry, your company and yourself.

Awards and credentials are great for demonstrating your expertise because they are often awarded by unbiased third parties who attest to your performance. Therefore, ensure you have awards and qualifications clearly shown or easily discoverable.

I recently had a client who was in a very competitive industry. They looked and operated in the same way as most of their competitors, and their competitive advantage was often achieved through price. I advised them that, rather than being generalists, each of their staff should have a speciality, something they knew the most about, thereby establishing them as an Authority. This allowed them to write about their niche in client newsletters, to speak about the topic at conferences and to interview industry experts and communicate this back to the organization and their clients. After a very short period of time, they didn't have to compete on price alone because they were the firm who had recognized industry experts working for them, and this was able to be clearly conveyed to their current and potential clients.

If you don't think you are an expert, neither will anyone else

One of the biggest failings I see in new persuaders is lack of confidence. Often, in a moment of nervousness, they will say things that erode their Authority. It is one thing to be humble, but if you doubt your own ability, you will struggle to persuade people in your direction. Therefore, study and master your craft. Find a mentor to guide you through and have faith that you know what you are talking about. If you do not know something, go and find it out.

Handoff

If your staff are struggling to establish their own Authority with a new client, stakeholder or partner, a handoff at the commencement of a meeting can assist. This is where you as the Authority introduce the team and highlight why they have been selected to lead or participate in the project. You can introduce their qualifications and expertise at the outset of a meeting much more easily than they are able to and to much greater effect.

This is also the reason why you should always have someone else introduce you when making speeches or at any form of public speaking engagement. Your introduction does not need to be long, but it does have to convey your expertise in the field so people know why they should listen to you.

It is much easier for someone else to say you know your stuff than it is for you to say so.

As an added bonus, if the person introducing you is an Authority in their space, this adds weight to their positive comments about you. Therefore, always strive for a senior, respected leader to introduce you to a group you haven't met.

Trust

Cialdini discovered through his research that being an expert on its own is not enough.[42] To be a credible Authority, you must also be able to be trusted. Trust, however, can take a long time to build, which, if you have time, is great because it also allows the relationship to form. If time is against you, a shortcut to achieving trustworthiness is to argue counter to your case or admit a weakness.[43]

The reason this is a shortcut is because only an Authority has the confidence to admit a weakness. It also disarms the persuadee because you are not just advocating the positives. In introducing a weakness, I am not talking about a cataclysmic failing (such as a pilot of a plane you have just boarded advising you that he has never flown this type of aircraft before but is excited to have a go!). Instead, it should be a minor weakness, and it must be accompanied by the word 'but', closely followed by a strong point highlighting your expertise.

For example,

> John, we have not completed a project with the exact specifications you have outlined, but we have done three other projects, two larger and one of equal size, and we know how to innovate in the design phase to help us return even greater savings and efficiencies than what you have asked for. Let me explain …

In the above example you have not tried to hide the weakness and then have provided a linked, positive point; this makes your already strong argument even stronger. If you don't admit your weaknesses, someone else will, and your credibility after that will be lost because you have hidden something and cannot be trusted. If you believe the persuadee thinks you have a weakness, it is a mistake to try to hide it. Address it early. If you get halfway through and have not disclosed the weakness, it is probably too late.

Apologize

If for some reason something goes wrong and it is your fault, apologize and apologize quickly. Only an Authority will apologize because they know they have the knowledge and skills to repair the damage or recover from whatever has occurred. However, make sure you follow your apology with a statement of how you intend to fix the situation.[44]

Putting it into writing

Wherever possible, bring your expertise to the surface in the documentation you provide to people who may not know you. Demonstrate your industry knowledge in the language and references you use.

Ensure your documents are well presented and are on heavier-weight paper with a colour or embossed logo. It has been shown that the weight of the paper and the effort that has gone into the design and printing conveys a message of being able to afford better quality stationery and, therefore, that you must be successful and *an* Authority.

It is worth noting that this thought process may or may not be conscious. For example, have you ever picked up a marketing document that was on lightweight paper, poorly printed and amateurish in design? Did it encourage you to do business with the person who gave it to you? Now, think about a glossy, well-printed document with great imagery, colour and design – entirely different, right? Before now, you probably never gave the paper a second thought.

The ultimate testament to your Authority is to write a book. It is not a coincidence that the etymology for 'author' and 'authority' is the same. However, consider the image you are seeking to convey with your book. Ebooks are easy to produce, but there is still something to be said in having a hard copy distributed in bookstores and online. They are also one of the best business cards you can hand a persuadee.

Presenting it

When presenting in front of people, speak clearly, confidently and convey your Authority through the terms and phrases you use. Do not rely on or use jargon that may confuse your audience, and never use words you do not know the meaning of.

As previously mentioned, have someone else introduce you and your expertise when meeting a group for the first time, and ensure the points in the introduction are relevant to the audience.

Using it online

In the digital realm, writing fresh and unique content can quickly establish you as an Authority. This can also be established by commenting on the blogs of existing Authorities, participating in joint ventures with them (such as webinars) and even interviewing them for presentation on your website to demonstrate your reach within the industry.

Wherever possible, have your products and services tested, certified and/or validated by independent third parties, and clearly post these results on your website or make it central to your brand if you need to convey an image of certainty through knowledge.

Post photos of you receiving awards, and make use of the digital files that are provided to you as a winner; add these to your signature block, stationery and website.

Beware

Beware the comments that you make online so as not to erode your Authority. Review your social and digital footprints regularly to ensure what others can see is a direct reflection and promotion of you as an Authority. A very simple tip is to open a browser in hidden or incognito mode (bypassing any cookies you may have in your browser history) and search for your name. Look at the images that come up and anything that may convey a negative message to a persuadee, such as an employer.

Beware those who seem too good to be true. As we saw in chapter 7 (see p. 34), Bernie Madoff had all the expertise to make him an Authority and, prior to his arrest, the trustworthiness. After reading this chapter, you can now see how Madoff used the trappings of Authority to lure people into his Ponzi scheme.

In 2012, Brett Cohen, a university student from New York, showed how easy it was to fake Authority. He went into Times Square with an entourage of security guards, aides, photographers and television crew. Cohen confidently walked around providing interviews, posing for photos and generally attracting the attention of passers-by. The pretend journalists then turned to the crowd to ask if they liked Cohen's films or his new single, none of which he had done. With all of these cues of Authority in place, fans scrambled for photos, autographs and to be near Cohen.[45]

The most interesting aspect of this stunt was how many people commented on his marvellous acting or singing ability, even though it was all a ruse.

Implications for you

- Apply for awards, write blogs and generally invest in yourself to ensure you are seen as an Authority.

- Promote your awards, qualifications and/or commendations from unbiased sources.

- Provide your credentials in advance of meetings.

- Assist with or request handoffs as necessary.

- Surround yourself with the trappings of an Authority.

- Apply the formula to tell others you can be trusted: admit any weaknesses that your persuadee may be concerned about; use 'but' as the all-important connector; and bring it home with a relevant, strong point.

- Beware false Authorities.

- Review your digital profile regularly to check for adverse comments.

- If you are not an Authority, identify someone who is and use their comments to add value to your argument.

- Remember, it is about being *an* Authority not *in* Authority.

23. Consistency

The principle of Consistency says that people are more willing to be moved in a particular direction if they see it as being consistent with an existing or recent commitment that they have made. Consistency aligns our beliefs, values and attitudes with what we have already done or decided.[46] As human beings we have a hardwired desire for Consistency. We despise hypocrisy and embrace those who do what they say, especially when times get tough.

Commitment and Consistency

In much of the persuasion literature, you will see the principle referred to as Commitment and Consistency. This is because to be Consistent you must have already made a Commitment.

 You have made an arrangement with a friend to meet them at a certain time for lunch. As the time draws near, you find yourself stuck in traffic. How do you feel?

Tense, uneasy, concerned? This is all driven out of our hardwired desire to remain consistent with the things we said we would do.

You contact your friend to tell them you will be fifteen minutes late due to traffic. Immediately the anxiety subsides, all because you have relieved yourself of the commitment you had previously made.

It is the Commitment that initiates the drive for Consistency.

It is important to realize that while Scarcity is an extrinsic motivator – the motivation to act is external to the persuadee – Consistency is an intrinsic motivator. It taps into the internal drivers to take action, usually based on preexisting beliefs, values and attitudes.

Active, public and voluntary Commitments

People seek to be Consistent with what they say, but they do so even more when they have made the Commitment publicly and it involves doing something, such as 'to become a workplace peer support officer'. In chapter 10, we saw the active nature of goals used in setting our Aim for our Persuasion Strategy; here, we are looking for people to make active commitments to do something and tell others about it.

Above all, the commitment must be voluntary. Samuel Butler said: 'He who complies against his will is of the same opinion still.'[47]

Therefore, create situations where the people you are attempting to influence are able to make comments about what they hope to achieve, their goals, their successes, their idea of failure. Ask them questions and allow them time to answer and commit to what they want.

The biggest mistake of many would-be persuaders is to make statements rather than ask questions. Making statements tells someone what you want them to; asking questions has them telling you what they will do.

Some academics have taken their knowledge of Consistency and turned it into an online business. StickK (www.stickk.com) is all about making Commitment contracts (online) to help people achieve their goals.

It is a simple, four step process:

1. **Set a goal:** What do you want to achieve and what time frame will you give yourself to achieve it?

2. **Set the stakes:** As an added incentive to succeed, you can wager an amount against your success. You nominate an amount and where it should go if you fail. You can then up the ante and place financial penalties upon yourself as punishment for not achieving milestones: a nice little introduction of Scarcity to keep you on track.

3. **Select a referee:** You nominate a referee, normally a friend or colleague, to monitor your progress and confirm the truth of your reports.

4. **Invite your friends and colleagues to support you:** This leverages the public aspect of commitment

making. If your friends don't know about your commitment yet, they soon will as you invite them to look over your shoulder.

This is a novel and great use of Consistency in the online world.

The same concept has enormous potential at home, work or even in social interactions with community groups, volunteers, etc. Make a game out of it, follow the steps and reap the rewards.

Do your research

Finding out what people stand for is critical to the persuasion process (see p. 45). If your persuadee has a deep-seated belief in a project, or they strongly reflect the company or their own personal values in what they do, then it makes sense to show how your proposal or request is aligned with those beliefs.

Researching previous projects, media releases, interviews, etc. can provide an insight into the person you are attempting to persuade. If you are unable to find personal commitments they have made, look to the values, vision and mission of the organization they work for. If they are a senior leader, it is very difficult to remain in a decision-making role if your personal values are not aligned with those of the organization you lead.

Use their momentum

A judo master does not look to exert enormous amounts of force on their opponents to win a match. Instead, they look to use the momentum and force of the opponent against them, guiding a strike past their own body and using this forward momentum to knock their opponent off balance. Consistency is much the same. It is much easier to use the persuadee's attitudes, values and beliefs to gain momentum and then simply guide them toward the desirable behaviour than to try to change their behaviour radically by force.

It is easy for me to resist you, but I tend not to resist myself.

The Thai Health Promotion Foundation advertisement 'Smoking Kid' depicts children asking adults who are smoking for a light for a cigarette. Every adult counsels the child about the dangers of smoking, after which the child hands the adult a note questioning the hypocrisy of their actions. Not one of the adults given the note throws it away. I would encourage you to watch the advertisement (which won numerous awards) as an example of understanding and leveraging Consistency (http://youtu.be/g_YZ_PtMkw0).

Change in attitude

One thing to be aware of when using Commitment and Consistency is to make sure the original Commitment is still held before relying upon it. For example, in 2010 the Australian campaigning group Get Up! targeted an advertisement at then Opposition Leader Tony Abbott. They had women of varying ages and ethnicities recount negative comments Abbott had made in the past about women and minority groups. The oldest comments came from 1974, and in the outro Mr Abbott was challenged as to whether he had changed.[48] While the saying goes 'a leopard doesn't change its spots', always ensure you check the Commitment is still current before raising it.

Putting it into writing

Signing contracts is a legal form of Commitment and Consistency that is enforceable through the courts. Social contracts are where you discuss someone's intended actions and have them write them down, such as setting performance goals for staff or identifying project milestones with team members. In these circumstances, it has been found that people tend to live up to what they write down.[49]

By way of example, I undertook a project with pharmacists who were tackling the issue of elderly patients forgetting to take their medication. Our solution was to have the pharmacist sit down to talk with the patient when they came in to get their prescription filled. They were asked:

- Do you know why the medication has been prescribed for you?

- Why do you think it's important that you take the medication?

- Have you ever forgotten to take the medication?

The pharmacist then passed the patient a blank piece of paper with the pharmacy logo on top and asked them to write down the requirements for their medication, e.g. 'take three tablets twice a day with food'. They then asked the patient what their normal routine was for taking their tablets. Identifying the location where they most commonly took their medication, the pharmacist then asked if they would stick the note in an obvious place near to where they normally took their medication. In every circumstance, the pharmacist waited for an answer to the question.

The pharmacy staff would call the patient later that day asking if they had any questions and if they had had a chance to place the reminder in the area they discussed with the pharmacist. Now, whenever the patient walked past the note saying 'take your medication', it was not the pharmacist or doctor saying they must take it, it was themselves. The consequence of patients making these active, public and voluntary Commitments was an immediate increase in medication compliance.

 When persuading upwards in the business (persuading those more senior than yourself), always offer to take the notes in a meeting. It provides you with the power of follow-up.

When disseminating the minutes of the meeting, make sure you list what was discussed and the associated action items. In the email to the leader, tell them you have recorded the action items and list them again in the body of the email. In closing, ask them if these action items are correct. In replying 'yes', they are also committing to each of the action items and the associated deadlines. Whenever time frames slip or milestones are missed, you simply need to enquire if priorities have changed. When they say 'no', highlight the agreed action items and allow their previous Commitment to bring them back into line with the project schedule.

Presenting it

Ask questions, don't make statements. Think about the commitment you are seeking and structure your question accordingly. Depending on the circumstances, when dealing with leaders and/or people from different cultures, always be mindful of allowing them to 'save face'. Sometimes the commitment is better obtained in smaller groups than in large gatherings.

Using it online

As we saw with StickK, Commitments can be elicited online. But, more broadly, think about your brand and what you are asking people to commit to on your website and in digital communications. If they can see their beliefs, values and attitudes in you and your brand, it is much easier for them to commit to you and remain committed. Therefore, do your research, draw the Implication and allow them to see how what you are proposing aligns with what they want.

TRY IT NOW!

Will you think about how you can trigger the principle of Consistency by asking others to make a Commitment?

Note that I started the above with 'Will you'. 'Will' is different to 'can' or 'could'. If someone says 'yes' to a 'Will you' question, they are committing actively and publicly to the action. If they say 'yes' to a 'Can you' question, they are saying 'yes I can', but it doesn't necessarily mean they will!

Assuming you said 'yes' to the above question, off you go: think about how you can use Consistency in your daily activities by soliciting a Commitment.

Implications for you

- Consistency is an intrinsic motivator – it uses the drive from within.

- Ask persuadees to nominate what they think is the best outcome.

- Ask them what they think the consequences should be if the result is not achieved.

- Wherever possible, have them write their Commitments down.

- Ask good questions, take good notes and, when projects start to drift, revisit the initial Commitments to ensure they are still valid. This will assist in getting back on track.

- When making Commitments, use technology, such as reminders in your calendar or phone, to keep yourself consistent. Mix up your reminders, perhaps setting a new one each week, so they don't become invisible and so you are continually making active Commitments to yourself.

24. Liking

We prefer to say 'yes' to people we know and like. For example, research has shown that at Tupperware home party demonstrations, guests are more likely to purchase a product because the host is a friend than out of their desire for the product itself.[50] In fact, the friend business model is so important to Tupperware that they ceased a commercial relationship with Target (a large American retailer) because Target's sales were too strong and were adversely impacting on their home demonstration model.[51] Tupperware understand the importance of relationships to their business success.

Liking is also critical in the formation of working relationships. By simply doing your research on a persuadee (as discussed in chapter 9) you will discover relevant info-nuggets that highlight what you have in common or something that you like about them. Sharing a fact you have discovered with your persuadee demonstrates you have taken the time to learn something about them and their business.

Building Liking

Similarity
We like people who are like us and, indeed, who like us. In 2010, research found that whom you get to know in your everyday life, where you live, your country of origin and

even social class provided stronger grounds for forging friendships than a just shared racial background.[52]

In dealing with individuals, take the time to discover things you have in common with them and uncover your shared goals. This is also true of groups, whether formal or informal.

Formal groups can be business units such as HR, operations or teams specifically formed to counter a particular problem.

Beneath the formal group structure is an informal one. The informal group is made up of people who have something in common – sporting interests, educational backgrounds, hobbies, enemies, etc. Informal groups can have a huge impact on the decision-making processes of individuals, groups and even organizations.

Individuals within the informal group share attributes, and they are drawn together because of them. Once they recognize these similarities in others in the group, the group itself develops an identity, it starts to function and Liking naturally occurs. Unlike many formal groups, the informal group is brought together and sustained by the similarities they share; they are not forced to find commonality to allow them to work together.

Take a lesson from the informal group. You do not need to force common attributes with others, especially similar values, beliefs and attitudes. People are like onions: they have many layers. You just need to find a layer on which you can connect.

Cooperation

If you are struggling to start a relationship with an individual, group or organization, pick a small task that you know you can't get wrong and cooperate on getting it done. During the process you will discover things you have in common and, inevitably, you will have done things for them, so Reciprocity is also now in play.

Once you complete the task, you will discover that working together is not so bad, and you will be able to praise each other genuinely for your activities.

The key is starting small and building up to the harder and more complex tasks. Just like picking teams in the schoolyard, when given the chance we prefer to work with people we know and like. Starting small and succeeding makes getting the persuadee to agree to a more complex task much easier.

Praise

Nothing builds the sense of Liking than delivery of genuine praise. If someone does something that is praiseworthy, tell them. If your business circumstances dictate that this is inappropriate, have someone else deliver your message and tell their colleagues, friends or leaders that they have done a great job. Everyone likes to be the bearer of good news, so your compliments will get back to the persuadee and, in turn, enhance your relationship with them.

Contrary to popular belief, it is impossible to make someone like you, but you can show them that *you* like *them*. The best way to do this is to tell them that you appreciate it when they ask good questions, turn up on time or drop off the documents they promised they would. Turn the language into collaborative positive language and watch the working environment change.

IF YOU REMEMBER ONE THING If you are struggling to form a relationship with a persuadee, identify a small task you can cooperate on, focus on your shared goals and praise them for the good work they do. Humanizing and taking time to work together builds relationships and friendships.

Validation

If you are looking for a quick visual story about praise, I would direct you to a short film called 'Validation'[53]. It tells a story about a parking attendant who gives his customers real validation. Not only does he validate their parking ticket, he also provides free compliments.

Director/writer Kurt Kuenne takes the principle of Liking and shows just how powerful praise and flattery can be. Kuenne also works an interesting sub-plot through the film, showing the effects on someone when they are not allowed to invest in another person, even though it is for genuine and selfless reasons. This shutdown closes off any opportunity for a relationship to build, as the door slams closed on Reciprocity. With Reciprocity, like begets like; when we are treated poorly we may return the disrespect with disrespect.

Putting it into writing

When writing emails, take the time to personalize the greeting. Invest in the relationship and allow people to see you like them. This is covered in more detail in chapter 26.

Presenting it

When speaking with people, listen to the things they have to say and identify the shared goals and similarities you have. Make time to invest in the relationship. When meeting someone for the first time, we are much more likely to comply with a request if we have shared a light dialogue first.

We can take a lesson from Chinese culture, where getting straight down to business and skipping the friendly interaction is considered impolite. Sharing information about your personal life, including family, hobbies, political views and even aspirations, allows the persuadee to see the similarities you share with them and to decide if they want a relationship with you and your business.

Using it online

Communicating online can make it difficult to connect with you personally. Therefore, in your 'about us' pages, provide some information that gives an insight into your personality and background. Sometimes it is easier to convey this via a video introduction on your website or making video calls than by relying on email and phone contact. All these efforts help to humanize you and provide a likeable face to the name.

 Think about someone you do not really get along with. Write down three positive things about them (they turn up on time, have nice handwriting, ask good questions, etc.).

Next time the situation arises where you encounter this positive behaviour, be sure to tell them.

If you choose not to, the relationship you have with them will never improve because it is unlikely that they will take the first step.

Implications for you

- Allow time to discuss the things you have in common with others.

- When you become aware of similarities, bring them to the surface to highlight the commonality.

- If your relationship with someone is not positive, look to ways you can cooperate with them on a small task and then genuinely praise them when it goes well.

25. Consensus

If you are walking down the street and a crowd is standing watching something, it is nearly impossible for you to look away. If, as you approach, the group starts running toward you screaming in horror, it is advisable you join them and run. If you get a video forwarded to you that has 2 million views, chances are you'll watch it. If you are travelling and need to find somewhere for dinner and you see two restaurants, one that is empty and one is full, chances are you'll go into the full one.

Why? These are all examples of Consensus, or Social Proof. The principle states that when we are not sure of what we should do, we look to the behaviour of others in that situation.

The example from chapter 4 of the UK Government's change in approach to getting people to pay their taxes on time (see p. 17) used Consensus. In the letter, the HMRC highlighted that most people in the area had already paid their taxes. Normalizing the positive behaviour (the timely payment of taxes) increased repayment rates by 15 per cent.[54]

Most like them

To move staff, get a key influencer from the staff on board by involving them in the project and have them engage, communicate with and move the group for you. In this case, the staff see themselves as more similar to their colleague so are more inclined to be persuaded by them than by management. If a teacher has a problem student in class, it is of little use having a peer leader talk to the child if they see themselves as totally different to that student. If the troublesome child is an athlete, then it makes most sense to have a student leader who is also an athlete talk to them about the virtues of knuckling down and working hard.

 When looking to shape the decisions of your persuadee, show them what people who are most like them are doing. For example, if you want to persuade a leader, show them what leaders like them are doing or have done in a similar situation.

If you are to show your persuadee what people like them are doing, you need to understand what that similar attribute is. Look for symmetry at a deeper level by observing how people like them have behaved in the past. Understanding this level of symmetry allows you to gain an understanding of how your persuadee may react.

While everyone is different, this will allow you to plan and reverse-engineer strategies based on the reactions of others like your persuadee. So, if you are in government and seeking to influence the behaviour of a member of the public, consider how members of the public like them have reacted before and plan for varying contingencies. If you are in the private sector, understand what has happened in previous fiscal or product cycles and what others did, to inform your strategies and how you might nudge your persuadee to do things differently.

Think of someone who is similar to your persuadee and who has exhibited the type of behaviour you are trying to get your persuadee to show. How can you highlight the behaviour of similar people in your presentation to them?

Inside their head

Getting inside your persuadee's head is not an easy task. They are an individual and are affected by different environmental and contextual factors that may have them react entirely differently to others, regardless of the level of symmetry.

This is where having a deeper understanding of their assets, resources, market position, capabilities, risks and liabilities will allow you to identify more than just one person, group or organization that is most like them. That way, should things not go the way you hoped, you can modify your approach and still present the one that will have the greatest impact on their decisions, and hopefully move them in the required direction.

You must realize, however, that even those most similar to your persuadee may not ultimately sway their decision because of the various other stakeholders, environmental and contextual factors that are at play.

Therefore, in anticipating the reactions of your persuadee – and ultimately developing a strategy to nudge them in your desired direction – you must consider the principle of Consensus on two levels:

- Organizational
- Individual.

Organizational

At the organizational level, you need to think like a strategist working for the organization. What does your persuadee need to do to convince others internally of the cultural, financial and/or environmental fit? By understanding their needs, you are better informed as to the similar 'others' to present; the situations that most closely reflect their current situation; and the broader implications your Persuasion Strategy has for them and their business.

You need to counter broad organizational uncertainty by providing Consensus examples at that level.

Individual

At the individual level, you need to understand who the Decision Maker is (as discussed in chapter 11).

Ensure that the Consensus data you are providing is targeted to them; this will ensure you get the biggest bang for your buck. For example, if you want a retail outlet to stock your product, is the persuadee the manager you speak to every visit, or is it the hands-off owner whom you've never met?

IF YOU REMEMBER ONE THING To influence decisions at the individual level, you need to know who the Decision Maker is and what they stand for. This will transition your data collection from mere collection to understanding.

Many others

The power of Consensus increases as the numbers do. For example, if one person is watching something, you will be less inclined to have a look than if a crowd is watching.

Use the power of many people through statistics, polls and surveys. The numbers to remember here are: one is an individual, two is a couple and three plus is 'many' and thus the tipping point.

Uncertainty

Consensus is most powerful when people are unsure about what they should do. It is at these times you want to highlight what others like them are doing in that or similar situations. Use statistics, testimonials or case studies to highlight the actions of others and allow these to guide your uncertain persuadee toward you.

Caution

A word of caution. Just as Consensus can have a positive impact by highlighting the positive or desired behaviour, highlighting the negative or unwanted behaviour can have a negative impact.

If you have a problem with staff turning up late to meetings, sending out an email saying 'It has been observed that a majority of staff are arriving late for meetings' will only serve to increase the numbers of people who are late. The timely attendees will say to themselves: 'Everyone else will be late so I'll turn up when everyone else does rather than waste my time.'

A study in the Petrified Forest National Park in the US highlighted that a well-intended sign stating 'Many past visitors have removed the petrified wood from the park, changing the natural state of the Petrified Forest' actually increased theft. In reality, less than 3 per cent of visitors took rocks, so a sign reading '97 per cent of guests leave the park as they found it' would have been more persuasive.[55]

Putting it into writing

Make use of polls, statistics and data that shows what many similar others are doing. One of the fastest and easiest ways to do this is to use infographics to clearly communicate what people are doing. As we saw in the Petrified Forest example be careful not to normalize undesirable behaviour though.

Written testimonials are extremely powerful because of the ability to show your persuadee what others just like them have done.

A written testimonial is persuasive. A written testimonial with the name and photo of the

182

person making the testimonial is better. A video testimonial is best.

Presenting it

If at all possible, obtain video testimonials from your clients. The reason video testimonials are so persuasive is because they are more genuine. You can see the person and the emotion they are conveying (or lack of it). If you coordinate a number of clients to come into your office or a studio to provide video testimonials, ensure you change the background (e.g. they aren't all sitting in front of the same painting), so it doesn't look as though the testimonials have been heavily constructed; this can erode the trustworthiness of the testimonial.

When speaking to others in person, use phrases like 'when we have done this with others' and 'others like you tend to …'. This gives the impression that others are doing and have done business with you, thereby reducing any uncertainty the persuadee may have.

If privacy and confidentiality are less of a concern, you may be able to name the organizations with whom you have worked. If confidentiality is a consideration, then using the pronoun 'we' may be sufficient to indicate you are doing or have done what you are proposing with others.

Using it online

Recent research shows that 84 per cent of people trust recommendations from a family member or friend, 69 per cent trust branded websites and 68 per cent trust consumer opinions posted online.[56] Therefore, wherever possible, collect customer feedback, reviews, statistics and data. Conduct surveys and allow people to interact with you socially (likes on Facebook, reviews on Yelp, ratings on eBay and so on). It all goes to convey that you are able to deliver what you say.

As with walking past a busy restaurant, if your website shows there are many people using your wares and working with you, it will attract more people. Potential customers will click and buy.

Implications for you

- Highlight what others like your persuadee are doing in a particular situation.

- Highlight what many others are doing in similar situations.

- Use Consensus when the persuadee is unsure or uncertain.

- Be careful to normalize desired, rather than undesired, behaviour.

- In presenting your Consensus data, understand that you thinking the persuadee is most like another individual, group or organization means nothing if they do not think they are similar.

26. Tips for persuading with email

We all know that persuading via email can be a struggle. So, how do we set about it? Let's review six easy steps to persuade with emails.

1. Have a cracker of a headline

The problem with many emails is that their subject line is cryptic and doesn't grab the attention of the persuadee. Those that answer the WIIFM question (see p. 80) will get a greater open rate, but if you don't know what subject lines are likely to get opened, test and measure. Try a couple of different approaches. For example, if I say: 'Here's your opportunity to seize an influx of resources' or 'Hey, I have £100 for you' which one would you open?

If you need to be a little more formal, provide your subject line with action words that can be easily identifiable in an inbox, such as:

FOR ATTENTION: Immediate Review of Budget
FOR APPROVAL: New Contract
REMINDER: Tender Submission Due Tuesday

Using reported facts from the media or headlines from the news shows the email is timely and perhaps includes something important or exclusive that the recipient may have missed (Scarcity):

Reserve Bank Drops Rates – Lisa, what it means for your mortgage

Media Regulation – the unintended impact on ABC Pty Ltd

 If you find a headline that works, don't use it over and over again. Test to find the ones that get the best reaction and change them regularly. Test new headlines and avoid becoming predictable. Over time, you will develop a suite of subject lines that command attention.

---

2. Make it personal

A study that looked at negotiations between college students found that those who started a negotiation task over email with no period of interaction – i.e. they got straight down to business – ended up in a stalemate 30 per cent of the time. Students who introduced themselves first – providing some personal details including their hobbies, their chosen field of study and their home town – stalled only 6 per cent of the time.[57] The negotiation task was exactly the same. The only difference was that the groups with the most successful completion rate were those who used Liking and personalized the interaction before getting down to business.

Therefore, even though you may be writing an email to a customer or a colleague, there is no excuse for it to be blunt, formal or boring. This goes for the headline and the body of the email too.

Write it as if you were writing to a friend. Don't use templates or long messages. Make comments at the outset that show you have made an effort for them and that this is not a generic email (see the next section – Give).

For example:

Hi Brian,

I hope you had a great weekend. We finally got some sunny weather and all that did was make it harder to come to work today.

The reason for my email is I read an article this morning and immediately thought of you. Have a look at paragraph three: it links perfectly with your current project.

www.socialinfluenceconsultinggroup.com.au/blog

Call me once you've read it as there are some nuances I want to walk you through so it doesn't cost you anything.

Speak soon,
Anthony

It has been shown that personal subject lines and messages can have twice the response rate of traditional messages; in some instances, they have even achieved a greater than 100 per cent increase in open rates over the standard approach.

Finally, sign the email. A personal signature, even a digital one, has a big impact on receptivity to your emails.

3. Give

In contacting your persuadees, think what is important to them. What will make their lives easier? Why would they continue to open and read your emails? Don't subject them to mass email blasts. Take the time to show them that you have made the effort to personally send them the email.

Give them content that is meaningful, customized and unexpected. This effort will drive reciprocation in effort and cultivate a working relationship in the process.

Remember though, that to be unexpected, you shouldn't give all the time (see p. 131). Be selective about who you share your information with and highlight its exclusive nature when this is the case. Give them what is truly valuable and they will give you business and loyalty, but you need to go first.

If you have a large database, then apply the 80/20 rule. For the 20 per cent of customers who give you 80 per cent of your revenue, personalize their messages. For the remainder, use a standard approach. If, however, one of your 80 per cent makes it into the top 20 per cent, tell them. Let them know you would like to provide a more personalized service because they are very important to you and let your emails reflect this.

 On a piece of paper, write down your most important clients, customers and stakeholders. These are the people and organizations you should be investing your time in. Write down one thing you can do differently for each to communicate to them how important they are to you.

---

4. Call to action

Your email should always have a call to action, making it clear what you want the persuadee to do. Whether it is in the subject line or in the body of the email, it must also always be in the final sentence.

Never create a call to action and then take them off on a different tangent, as the call to action will be lost.

> Hi Jill,
>
> I am really looking forward to your briefing on Thursday.
> In preparation for the meeting, can you please provide a copy of the presentation for the leadership team no later than 2pm on Wednesday, along with a short video synopsis explaining your take on the current staff leave policy?
> I hope your new team is performing well and really embracing the new technology platforms we have introduced. It is making a big difference to other parts of the business.
>
> John

The final comment about technology can open the door for a conversation on that issue, taking attention away from the actual focus of the email that was introduced in paragraph two – the company's leave policy.

Always leave the reader primed to carry out the action

you have requested. If the action is asking for business, I would recommend not doing it over email because if they say 'no' it is harder for you to make a concession, thereby reducing the chances they will make a concession and accept your BATNA (see p. 130).

5. Time your email

Sometimes the greatest decider of your email being opened and action being taken is the time of day or night it is sent. The best indicator is to review when your persuadee has most frequently opened and/or replied to emails in the past.

Failing that, research on over one billion emails identified the following information, which you can use to guide your timing:[58]

- The top time of day for emails is 2–5pm.
- Tuesday and Thursday are the highest volume email days.
- New recipients are the most engaged.

Furthermore, we also know that emails have the greatest open and action rates in the first hour after they are sent. Therefore, when sending important emails, ensure you send them in the hour prior to the above listed times. Depending on the recipient's schedule, also consider early mornings if they come in early so the email is waiting for them when they arrive. Alternatively, early afternoon ensures they have had the majority of the day to clear existing issues and have time to reflect on your request. Ultimately test, test, test.

When emails are received after 8pm they may get opened, but if you are asking for considerable action, it may be held over until the following day; then, in the morning the newer emails are sitting on top of yours, perhaps rendering it to inbox oblivion.

6. Review

Finally, you must review your efforts and ensure that the strategy employed is achieving the desired results. If it doesn't, ask why not? What can you improve for next time?

Create a folder on your computer or server called 'Swipe File'. Whenever you come across a good headline or receive an email from someone that made you jump or in which the body content was crystal clear, save a copy to your Swipe File for later reference.

Implications for you

- Use persuasive headlines.
- Make it personal to the persuadee.
- Give things that are important to them.
- Use clear calls to action as the last thing in the email.
- Time your email for optimal opening, attention and action.
- Review your efforts and test and measure frequently.

27. Emotion versus logic

One of the most common errors I see in persuasion activities where people observe the lessons but do not learn from them is the mistaken belief that emotion can be countered with logic. While Aristotle believed an audience could be persuaded by a speaker's character (*ethos*), the reasoning of their argument (*logos*) and their passion (*pathos*), he was cognisant of the persuadee and the application of these elements.

In chapter 12, we looked at the 'why' for the persuadee and the importance of understanding their motivation and reasons for doing things. In chapter 13, we looked at the intensity of their attitude and the importance of understanding where we start from in our persuasive endeavours.

The science of emotion has been well researched and is clearly linked to the field of persuasion.

 Emotion countered with logic alone will fail every time.

Colour of emotion

To help us explore this further, let's consider persuasion and emotion through colours. If the persuadee is prone toward one colour/emotion, then they can move further into that colour during the persuasion encounter, unless the emotion is dealt with.

Red/Anger

Red is the persuadee who is irritated and may tend toward anger. This person may be looking for a fight, or may feel their goals have been obstructed in some way or that they are being dealt with unjustly.[59]

If a persuadee is Red about the proposal or situation – and if the source of the anger is not addressed – they may become angrier and react against the proposal. The persuader needs to recognize that the persuadee feels their goals are being obstructed and/or they are being dealt with unjustly and neutralize the Red.

Dealing with Red:

- **Reciprocity**: Validate the emotion. Recognize they are upset and give them the opportunity to voice this anger.

- **Consensus**: Show them that others are in a similar position and it is not just them.

- **Authority**: Use an independent expert to provide guidance to an outcome rather than tell them they are wrong.

Never tell the persuadee to calm down or that they are wrong – this invalidates the emotion of anger and will make it worse!

Blue/Sadness

Blue is the persuadee who is experiencing sadness, has frozen or has just given up on the situation. In this state they are looking for assistance or help.[60]

If the persuadee feels sad about the current situation and options are not provided to help them recover or move past the blockage, the situation could simply become worse and your persuasion attempts will go largely ignored as the persuadee becomes preoccupied with the loss and trying to avoid it.

Dealing with Blue:

- **Mitigate Scarcity**: Recognize they are sad and provide clear steps on how to avoid the loss they are feeling. Saying 'I'm sorry for your loss' does little to help them overcome it.

- **Reciprocity**: Provide them with assistance in dealing with the issue.

- **Liking**: Praise the good work they have done so far.

- **Liking**: Offer to cooperate on the task with them.

Green/Fear

Green is the persuadee who is experiencing fear or anxiety and is looking to avoid physical or psychological harm.[61] If not dealt with, the persuadee may become increasingly fearful or anxious, moving into a mode of freeze (do nothing), fight (react against you) or flight (run away, hide and do nothing).

Dealing with Green:

- **Reciprocity**: Recognize they are fearful.

- **Framing**: Show them it is not as bad as other situations.

- **Consensus**: Show them they are not the only one to have gone through this.

- **Authority**: Highlight what others with greater experience or wisdom suggest.

- **Mitigate Scarcity**: Draw attention to the further losses that will occur if they freeze and do nothing.

Orange/Happy

Orange is the persuadee who is achieving their goals and is happy. This makes moving toward their future goals easier. While anger, sadness and fear may attract your attention, it is just as important to recognize an Orange. By recognizing that the persuadee is happy and feels they are progressing toward their goals, you are better able to identify their motivators and hot buttons, what drives them to do certain things.

Dealing with Orange:

- **Liking**: Provide them with genuine thanks and praise for their efforts.

- **Reciprocity/Liking**: Offer to assist them further.

- **Liking**: Highlight that you have similar goals.

- **Liking**: Tell them you like them and working with them.

- **Consistency/Mitigate Scarcity**: Get an acknowledgment from them that with alternative participants or methods it may not have turned out so well.

 Think of a persuadee you are currently dealing with and link their situation as per the colour above and identify your next steps in dealing with them.

Implications for you

In persuading others, we need to deal with the emotion that is driving the negative behaviour or the behaviour to be changed.

The process for doing this is:
- Recognize the emotion/colour.

- Interpret what it means.

- React – neutralize, diffuse or reinforce the emotion as required.

SECTION 4:
Lessons learned

In the preceding chapters we have discussed many ideas and approaches to persuasion. The question is: how successful will you be? Will you put this book down and act upon what you have read, or will you put it on the shelf and do what you have always done?

To be truly persuasive you need to have an idea of your strengths and weaknesses. You also need know what works in your space and what doesn't.

28. Review the outcome and process

Rather than focusing on outcome alone, we should review the outcome *and* the process:

- Good process with a positive outcome = High quality

- Flawed process with a positive outcome = False positive

- Flawed process with a poor result = Low quality

- Good process with a poor result = False negative

Using the science of persuasion is not an ironclad guarantee because we are dealing with people. Sometimes you will succeed because you planned and executed well. Other times you will plan and execute well but, despite your best efforts, the persuadee is reacting against you, the situation or some other factor. Recognizing that you have done everything you can is very important.

 If we just review our performance on outcome alone, those who persuade by luck or intuition think they are highly successful, yet they don't know what works and struggle to replicate it when needed because they don't understand the process.

Those who focus on outcome alone and take a

confidence hit because of an unsuccessful result may miss the fact that they gave it all they had.

We would love to succeed every time, but false positives are dangerous, and many would-be persuaders live on these successes until it is too late. Recognizing a false negative for what it is is just as important as succeeding – this is what develops the knowledge and skills of a persuader beyond luck or intuition.

Be genuine in your approach, research your persuadee well, try as hard as you can and, when your efforts succeed, celebrate. Equally though, when an approach doesn't work, review the process to identify why not and continue to develop your skills.

 It is not enough to simply observe the lessons. You must learn from each and every persuasion endeavour you undertake and learn from any failures. Identify how you can better plan or execute in the future, thereby avoiding the same mistakes happening again.

Learning from rejection

Just the mention of the word 'rejection' triggers a reaction in our limbic brain. Our emotional control centre starts searching for the appropriate response: fight, flight or freeze.

However, rejection is one of the best sharpening stones for our persuasive ability. When you get rejected, don't drop your bundle. Instead, think 'What could I have done differently?'

We have heard it before, but Tim Ferriss – author of *The 4-Hour Workweek* – was rejected 26 times before a publisher said 'yes'; Stephen King was rejected 30 times before *Carrie* was accepted; and we all know that J.K. Rowling heard many rejections before Harry Potter finally got his wand out at Hogwarts.

What, therefore, can we learn from a rejection?

It is insane not to learn from being rejected

If you get a 'no', don't do the same thing you have always done and expect a different outcome.

Break it down. Look at your approach. Look at the tools you used and find out why you missed the mark.

If you win, you need to know why. If you lose, you need to know why. The important thing is that you need to have a process to fall back on to turn the 'no' into a longer-term success.

Ultimately, if you are getting rejected, ask why.

It is a sign that something needs to be fixed, something about your letter of introduction, your pitch, your offer or your website. It's broken, so ask what you could have done differently and fix it. Change one variable at a time so you can test and measure success.

The secret sauce

But also think of rejection as your own special sauce. The secret ingredients that will make your requests better than they ever have been before.

You can guarantee that you are not the only one getting rejected, but how you deal with it will set you apart.

If others get rejected and drop out of the race, it means there is more opportunity for you.

If you missed the mark, ask the Decision Maker for feedback on how you could have improved. If you missed out to a competitor, ask how you could have approached it differently. The answers you will get will give you an insight into the Decision Maker's thought processes and will give you the blueprint for future persuasive appeals.

Aha!

Rejection is feedback telling you that you are not quite there yet. Each time you get feedback, learn from it, and you will get closer to the right ingredients to get to yes.

The other upside is when you get a rejection, it gives you time to focus on things you are good at and refine that to a higher degree.

Finally, if someone tells you 'no', it may be that they were not the right client for you anyway!

If you have received a rejection recently, approach the Decision Maker for some feedback. If you are not sure if they will tell you, make it about them, not you. Tell them that if you get an idea of where you missed the mark you will be better prepared to give them what they want in future projects or presentations.

Implications for you

- When assessing your persuasiveness, review the outcome and the process used.

- There are no guarantees with persuasion, so you must learn what works and what doesn't work and why.

- Learn from rejection, don't run away from it.

- Ask why, modify your approach and try again.

- Think of rejection as your own special sauce. It is the one ingredient that will make your persuasive appeals better.

29. A closing word: test and measure everything

With everything that has been suggested in this book, you must test and measure. Take nothing for granted. Change just one variable at a time until you understand where the 'secret sauce of persuasion' lies for your persuadee.

You will experience success early and will be tempted to stop your testing and just employ your new found technique. I encourage you to test a little longer rather than change all of your processes based on a single or limited number of successes. You need to understand why the change occurred; do not simply be satisfied with it occurring.

Above all, be brave. Be willing to make mistakes. If you do, you will be willing to give things a go. If you fear mistakes and seek only perfection, you will be condemned to mirror the actions of others and never truly innovate or understand why things work.

Anything is possible. If you take what you have learned in this book, hearing 'yes' will be far more likely than it was before you read it.

Acknowledgements

Thanks to Bob Cialdini, Bobette Gorden, Gregory Neidert and Eily VanderMeer from Influence at Work for their ongoing friendship and support. Thanks to my sister Andrea and mother Margaret for providing commentary on the manuscript. To my father Robert for his inspiration and to my close friends and thought leaders Mel Dunn, Brian Ahearn, Niamh Shuley, James Dakin, Peter Eichmann, Steve Longford, Murray Rankin, Lawrence Symonds, Nick Lehmann, Ben Nielsen and Brett and Melissa Ambrose. A big thanks to every person who has ever attended one of my workshops, asked questions or discussed persuasion with me.

Endnotes

1. Duhigg, C. (2012) *The Power of Habit: Why We Do What We Do in Life and Business*. New York: Random House.

2. Gardner, H. (2006) *Changing Minds. The Art and Science of Changing Our Own and Other People's Minds*. Boston: Harvard Business School Press.

3. Carnegie, D. (1936) *How To Win Friends and Influence People*. New York: Simon and Schuster.

4. McDougall, W. (1908) *An Introduction to Social Psychology*. London: Methuen & Co.

5. Milgram, S. (1963) 'Behavioral study of obedience'. *Journal of Abnormal and Social Psychology*, 67, 371–378.

6. Zimbardo, P.G. (1971) *Stanford Prison Experiment*. Stanford University.

7. Cialdini, R.B. (1993) *Influence: The Psychology of Persuasion* (Revised edition). New York: Quill.

8. Coleman, S. (1996) *The Minnesota Income Tax Compliance Experiment: State Tax Results*. Minnesota Department of Revenue. Also: Hallsworth, M., List, J.A., Metcalfe, R. & Vlaev, I. *The Behavioralist as Tax Collector: Using Natural Field Experiments to Enhance Tax Compliance* (March 2014) NBER Working Paper No. w20007. Available at SSRN: http://ssrn.com/abstract=2418122.

9. Schultz, P.W., Nolan, J.M., Cialdini, R.B., Goldstein, N.J. & Griskevicius, V. (2007) 'The constructive, destructive and reconstructive power of social norms'. *Psychological Science*, 18: 429–434.

10. Thaler, R.H. & Sunstein, C.R. (2008) *Nudge: Improving Decisions about Health, Wealth and Happiness*. New Haven: Yale University Press.

11. *Behavioural Insights Team: Annual Update 2010–11*. London: Cabinet Office.

12. Aronson, E. (1999) *The Social Animal* (8th ed). New York: Worth Publishers.

13. Simons, H.W. & Jones, J.G. (2011) *Persuasion in Society* (2nd ed.) New York: Routledge.

14. Cialdini, R.B. (2012) *Principles of Persuasion Workshop*. Arizona: Influence at Work.

15. Fishman, S. (2011) 'The Madoff Tapes'. *New York Magazine*.

16. Doran, G.T. (1981) 'There's a S.M.A.R.T. way to write management's goals and objectives'. *Management Review*, Vol. 70, Issue 11(AMA FORUM), pp. 35–36.

17. Lindsay, G. (2014) 'Relationship science: harnessing big data for power networking'. *Inc Magazine*. April edition.

18. Drozdeck, S., Yeager, J. & Sommer, L. (1991) *What They Don't Teach You in Sales 101*. New York: McGraw-Hill.

19. Huczynski, A. (1996) *Influencing within Organizations: Getting in, Rising up, and Moving on*. Harlow: Prentice Hall.

20. Cherry, K. 'Theories of motivation: a closer look at some important theories of motivation'. *About.com*. http://psychology.about.com/od/psychologytopics/tp/theories-of-motivation.htm. Accessed 13/08/14.

21. Gass, R. & Seiter, J. (2007) *Persuasion, Social Influence, and Compliance Gaining* (3rd ed.) Boston: Allyn & Bacon.

22. Simons, H.W. & Jones, J.G. (2011) *Persuasion in Society* (2nd ed.) New York: Routledge.

23. *Ibid.*

24. *Ibid.*

25. Sinek, S. (2009) *Start with Why: How Great Leaders Inspire Everyone to Take Action*. New York: Portfolio Penguin.

26. Grant Pearson Brown Consulting. http://www.gpb.eu/2009/09/the-fbi-pushes-our-hot-cold-buttons-so-what.html. Accessed 13/08/14.

27. Simons, H.W. & Jones, J.G. (2011) *Persuasion in Society* (2nd ed.) New York: Routledge.

28. Jones, P. (2012) *Get it Write*. Magneto Communications. http://www.magneto.net.au/writing-courses.html.

29. Social Influence Consulting Group blog.
    http://socialinfluenceconsultinggroup.com.au/my-inability-to-skim-rocks.

30. Carnegie, D. (1936) *How To Win Friends and Influence People*. New York: Simon and Schuster.

31. www.influenceatwork.com

32. Cialdini, R.B. (2009) *Influence: Science & Practice* (5th ed). USA: Pearson Education.

33. Strohmetz, D.B., Rind, B., Fisher, R. & Lynn, M. (2002) 'Sweetening the till: the use of candy to increase restaurant tipping'. *Journal of Applied Social Psychology*, 32: 300–309.

34. Goldstein, N.J., Martin, S.J. & Cialdini, R.B. (2008) *Yes!: 50 Scientifically Proven Ways to Be Persuasive*. New York: Free Press.

35. Grant, A. (2013) *Give and Take: A Revolutionary Approach to Success*. London: Weidenfeld & Nicolson.

36. Garner, R. (2005) 'Post-it Note persuasion: a sticky influence'. *Journal of Consumer Psychology*, 15: 230–237

37. Mauss, M. (1954) *The Gift*. London: Cohen and West.

38. Gilovich, T. & Medvec, V.H. (1995) 'The experience of regret: what, when, and why'. *Psychological Review*. Vol. 102: 379–395.

39. Kinnier, R.T. & Metha, A.T. (1989) 'Regrets and priorities at three stages of life'. *Counseling and Values*. Vol. 33: 182–193.

40. https://www.youtube.com/watch?v=gCMzjJjuxQI

41. Weingarten, G. (2007) 'Pearls before breakfast'. *Washington Post*. 8 April 2007.

42. Cialdini, R.B. (2009) *Influence: Science and Practice* (5th ed.) Boston: Pearson Education.

43. Goldstein, N.J., Martin, S.J. & Cialdini, R.B. (2008) *Yes!: 50 Scientifically Proven Ways to Be Persuasive*. New York: Free Press.

44. *Ibid.*

45. Chaney, J. (2012) 'Brett Cohen: the New Yorker who pretended to be

famous and is now a little famous because of it'. *Washington Post.* 23 August 2012.

46. Simons, H.W. & Jones, J.G. (2011) *Persuasion in Society* (2nd ed.) New York: Routledge.

47. Butler, S. with notes by T.R. Nash (1835). *Hudibras.* Oxford: Oxford University Press.

48. Get Up! Australia (2010) 'Tony Abbott's archaic views'. http://youtu.be/pJTX0iWYX9A. Accessed 21/06/14.

49. Cialdini, R.B. (2009) *Influence: Science & Practice* (5th ed.) Boston: Pearson Education.

50. Frenzen, J.K. & Davis, H.L. (1990) 'Purchasing behavior in embedded markets'. *Journal of Consumer Research.* Vol. 17: No 1 (June): 1–12.

51. Brooks, R. (2004) 'A deal with target put lid on revival at Tupperware'. *The Wall Street Journal.* 18 February 2004.

52. Wimmer, A. & Lewis, K. (2010) 'Beyond and below racial homophily: ERG models of a friendship network documented on Facebook'. *American Journal of Sociology.* Vol 16: No 2. September 2010: 583–642.

53. Kuenne, K. (2007) 'Validation'. http://youtu.be/Cbk980jV7Ao.

54. *Behavioural Insights Team: Annual Update 2010–11.* London: Cabinet Office.

55. *Ibid.* (pp. 21–23).

56. Nielsen (2013). *Global Trust in Advertising and Brand Messages,* Q3.

57. Cialdini, R.B. (2012) *Principles of Persuasion Workshop.* Arizona: Influence at Work.

58. Mailchimp (2014) 'Find your best sending times'. *Genome Project.*

59. Ekman, P. (2003). *Emotions Revealed: Recognizing Faces and Feelings to Improve Communication and Emotional Life.* New York: Times Books.

60. *Ibid.*

61. *Ibid.*

Index

INTRODUCING GRAPHIC GUIDES

Covering subjects from Quantum Theory to Wittgenstein, Sociology to Islam and much more, the Graphic Guides use comic-book style illustrations to deftly explain humanity's biggest ideas.

'INTRODUCING is a small miracle of contemporary publishing ... Buy one now. Feel smarter almost immediately.' Don Paterson, *Guardian*

introducingbooks.com

facebook.com/ introducingbooks